C000124606

DUDLEY

THE TWENTIETH CENTURY

THE BLACK COUNTRY SOCIETY

This voluntary society, affiliated to the Civic Trust, was founded in 1967 as a reaction to the trend of the late 1950s and early 1960s to amalgamate everything into large units and in the Midlands to sweep away the area's industrial heritage in the process.

The general aim of the Society is to create interest in the past, present and future of the Black Country, and early on it campaigned for the establishment of an industrial museum. In 1975 the Black Country Museum was started by Dudley Borough Council on 26 acres of totally derelict land adjoining the grounds of Dudley Castle. This has developed into an award-winning museum which attracts over 250,000 visitors annually.

At the Black Country Museum there is a boat dock fully equipped to restore narrow boats of wood and iron and different boats can be seen on the dock throughout the year. From behind the Bottle and Glass Inn visitors can travel on a canal boat into Dudley Canal Tunnel, a memorable journey to see spectacular limestone caverns and the fascinating Castle Mill Basin.

There are over two thousand members of the Black Country Society and all receive the quarterly magazine *The Blackcountryman*, of which over 119 issues have been published since its founding in 1967. In the whole collection there are some 1,700 authoritative articles on all aspects of the Black Country by historians, teachers, researchers, students, subject experts and ordinary folk with an extraordinary story to tell. The whole constitutes a unique resource about the area and is a mine of information for students and researchers who frequently refer to it. Many schools and libraries are subscribers. Three thousand copies of the magazine are printed each quarter. It is non-commercial, and contributors do not receive payment for their articles.

PO Box 71 · Kingswinford · West Midlands DY6 9YN

DUDLEY

THE TWENTIETH CENTURY

HILARY ATKINS, DIANE MATTHEWS & SAMANTHA ROBINS

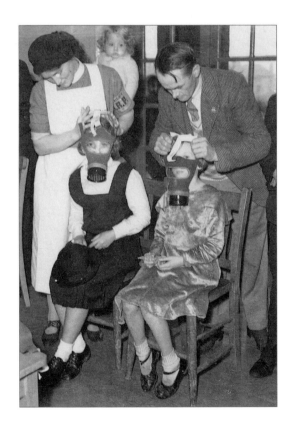

SUTTON PUBLISHING

First published in the United Kingdom in 1999 by
Sutton Publishing Limited · Phoenix Mill
Thrupp · Stroud · Gloucestershire · GL5 2BU

Copyright © Hilary Atkins, Diane Matthews & Samantha Robins, 1999

All rights reserved. No part of this publication may be reproduced, stored in a retrieval system, or transmitted, in any form or by any means, electronic, mechanical, photocopying, recording or otherwise, without the prior permission of the publisher and copyright holder.

Hilary Atkins, Diane Matthews & Samantha Robins have asserted the moral right to be identified as the authors of this work.

British Library Cataloguing in Publication Data
A catalogue record for this book is available from the British Library.

ISBN 0-7509-2212-5

The photographs and other material included here are a very small selection from the collections held by Dudley Archives and Local History Service, Mount Pleasant Street, Coseley, which include 17,000 photographs and several hundred thousand other items, covering the area of the present Metropolitan Borough of Dudley. The Service is always interested to hear from anyone who would be prepared to loan or give any other material.

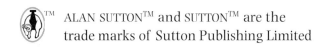
ALAN SUTTON™ and SUTTON™ are the trade marks of Sutton Publishing Limited

Typeset in 11/14pt Photina.
Typesetting and origination by
Sutton Publishing Limited.
Printed in Great Britain by
Redwood Books, Trowbridge, Wiltshire

Contents

Members of Dudley Police Force outside the police station, Priory Street, by night, lit by one of the electric street lights, 1936.

Introduction

The twentieth century has been a period of great change the world over. This book attempts to illustrate how these changes have affected one small Midlands town, and how that town has contributed to events which have shaped the country and the world.

There has been a settlement at Dudley since early times, and the name itself is probably of Saxon origin. Dudley Castle still stands today in testament to the town's medieval history. A market was granted to Dudley in the twelfth century, and by this time also the town could boast two churches, St Thomas's to serve the town, and St Edmund's to serve the castle community, and a Cluniac priory, whose ruins can be seen today in Priory Park. Despite this, very few national events touched Dudley, with the exception of the Civil War, until the nineteenth century.

Dudley, with its many accessible natural resources, found itself at the centre of the Industrial Revolution, and became a major manufacturing centre, exporting goods all over the world. While the town's wealth was reflected in many new civic buildings in the last century, such as the town hall, police station, free library and art gallery, the working population lived in poverty, in slum housing built in the courts and yards of the medieval burgage plots which lined the streets leading to the castle. The Earl of Dudley still had great influence in the town. He still wholly owned the castle and grounds at the turn of the century, but allowed public access to the grounds for pleasure, and once a year hosted fêtes there, at Whitsun. He was also a generous benefactor to the town, building a new town hall in Priory Street, giving the site for Netherton library, and in 1867 providing the fountain which still stands in Market Place. At the turn of the century, then, Dudley was a vigorous industrial town, enjoying the relative peace and prosperity of the times, but overcrowded and still retaining something of the look of a medieval town, in structure, despite its newer civic buildings and some new roads.

The twentieth century began, much as the nineteenth century ended, with the country stable and prosperous, and Queen Victoria still on the throne. The first chapter here has been called 'Edwardian Dudley', although it actually covers the last year of Queen Victoria's reign, and the first years of King George V's. Britain was involved, in the first years of the century, in the Boer War, and although people at home followed its progress with great interest and concern, it was more akin to the colonial wars of the nineteenth century than the devastating world wars of the twentieth. In 1914 Dudley, along with the rest of the country, waved her sons off to the First World War – many of them would not return, and many who did were dreadfully wounded. On the home front, Dudley people rallied around for war charities, to help prisoners of war, wounded soldiers and European refugees; many women took jobs in munitions factories, such as the National Projectile Factory in Dudley, and a new threat was born – the air raid.

The end of the war, was, understandably, a cause for much celebration, but the years that followed brought more turbulent times, with industrial unrest, the General Strike, and the Great Depression. The 1930s also saw a rise in international tension, which would eventually culminate in the Second World War. It is hard to overestimate the impact of this war on Britain, and here the chapter 'War and Peace' illustrates some of the effects it had on Dudley and her people, and the beginnings of recovery in the immediate post-war years. Before the war had even broken out, gas masks had been distributed to civilians and trenches dug, and before long it seemed that most of the population was in uniform. The blackout and the threat of air raids were part of everyday life until after the D-Day landings of 1944, and the relief at the end of the war in 1945 led once again to spontaneous celebrations. In the aftermath of war rationing continued and austerity was the order of the day. Britain's war-ravaged cities were being rebuilt, and the need for additional housing led even towns like Dudley, which had escaped relatively unscathed, to undertake building schemes.

The 1950s and '60s brought greater affluence for more people than ever before. At the end of the '50s the Prime Minister Harold Macmillan said 'most of our people have never had it so good' and this held true for much of the following decade as well. Meanwhile, Britain was losing her Empire, on which before the war 'the sun had never set', and making her first attempt to join the EEC. They were also decades when a definable youth culture began to emerge for the first time, and young people developed their own fashions and musical tastes. Dudley changed in appearance more, perhaps, during these decades than at any other time. Many old buildings were demolished and replaced. In their place, tower blocks and modern shopping precincts of concrete and glass sprang up. The optimism of this period, however, was not to last long. The 1970s and '80s brought a decline in the heavy, manufacturing industries on which Dudley had traditionally relied and unemployment hit levels not seen since the 1930s. At the same time technology was advancing apace, particularly in the field of computers and information technology, and some of the associated high-tech industries have been located in this area.

The twentieth century has seen a major transport revolution, from horse-drawn vehicles to the huge proliferation in motor transport, and from biplanes to the space age. At the turn of the century motor cars were very much the preserve of the rich, but with mass production and greater prosperity became an essential of modern life. The effects are well known – pollution and traffic congestion, and on the other hand, the freedom to live further from work and the advent of the out-of-town shopping centre. All of these have affected Dudley in some ways. Road improvements became necessary as early as the 1920s, largely because of the influence of motor vehicles, and continue today. Roads have had to be widened, leading to the loss of many older buildings; monuments have been moved or removed, if they caused obstructions to vehicles; new traffic calming and control methods have been implemented, and new roads built. The latest of these, Dudley Southern Bypass, opened in October 1999, five months ahead of schedule. At the same time, the number of people actually living in the old town centre has declined, and the Merry Hill centre in Brierley Hill has been a huge success, to the detriment of older centres like Dudley.

This has also been a century of social and political change. In 1900 most working men and all women were denied the vote. The twentieth century has seen not only universal suffrage but also the first Labour government, and, in 1979, the first woman prime minister. Dudley elected its first female councillor in 1933 and its first lady mayor, Dr Kate Rogers, in 1971. More jobs have been opened up to women, and an Equal Opportunities Commission established. This century has also seen the beginning of free secondary education for all, after the 1944 Education Act, and the school leaving age increased from twelve to sixteen. Since the 1960s comprehensive secondary education has become the norm and in Dudley the 400-year-old grammar school and the Girls' High School ceased to be selective in the 1970s. The end of the workhouse system, in the 1920s, and the birth of the welfare state and the National Health Service in the 1940s have dramatically altered the quality of life of many. One of the greatest social changes has been the growth of ethnic minority communities in Britain, particularly since the Second World War. Initially many men, particularly from the Indian subcontinent and the West Indies, came to Britain to take up jobs which could not be filled in the postwar years. By the early 1980s, 4.5 per cent of Dudley borough's population was from ethnic minority groups, and this has remained more or less static.

Leisure time has increased over the century, with a shorter working week and paid holidays, leading to the provision of more recreational facilities, such as swimming baths, parks, skating rinks, and, in Dudley, the zoo. Dudley Opera House opened in 1900, and was followed by several other smaller variety theatres, most of which later became cinemas. Cinema-going was probably at its most popular between the wars, but as televisions became more commonplace in the home, and later home videos became available, numbers declined and cinemas closed. The last cinema to be built in Dudley was the Odeon in Castle Hill, which opened in 1937 and closed in 1975, and the Plaza was the last to close in 1990. Dudley currently has no cinema, but one is planned as part of the Castle Gate development, and is due to open soon in the next century.

As we near the end of the twentieth century Dudley can look back on a very turbulent time. It has come through two world wars, a Great Depression and more recent recession, and has changed enormously in the process. Dudley today is a modern, multi-cultural town, which has become less industrial, and whose residents have tended to move out of the town centre on to its fringes. As Dudley's inhabitants look forward to the new century, the transformation of their town continues with the opening of the Dudley Southern Bypass, the planned Castle Gate complex, and the building of several thousand new houses during the next ten years. The town also honoured one of its most famous sons, Duncan Edwards, when his statue was unveiled in the Market Place in October 1999.

1. Edwardian Dudley

Dudley Market Place, *c.* 1900, looking towards Castle Street and St Edmund's church with Hall Street on the right with the tramlines and horses and carts. The eighteenth-century buildings can be seen above the shop fronts. The shop on the corner of Hall Street is S. Sheward, the Midland Meat Store. His advertisements in Blocksidge's *Dudley Almanack* and the *Dudley Herald* read as follows: 'The Greatest Wonder in the Midland Counties is the Quantity of Meat Always Shewn at the Corner of Hall Street Dudley. Also the Quality and Price.'

Introduction

People who saw the dawn of the new century in January 1900 thought that it would be one of peace, progress and prosperity, and that things would continue as they had in the preceding century. Queen Victoria was still on the throne, having reigned for sixty-three years. In fact Dudley does not seem to have officially celebrated the birth of the new century although there were perhaps private and individual celebrations. Indeed the mayor in wishing the corporation a happy new year at the first meeting of the century on 2 January, added that he did not think they should debate the knotty problem of whether they were in fact entering a new century!

The end of an era and the beginning of the Edwardian age came with the death of Queen Victoria on 22 January 1901. This, the proclamation of Edward VII as king and the queen's funeral were marked in Dudley with public mourning and memorial services. The coronation of the king was, however, postponed because of his serious illness and did not take place until 1902, when Dudley celebrated along with the rest of the country. Edward died in 1910, and his son was crowned George V in 1911. The country went through the process of mourning and celebration once again and Dudley was no exception. It is perhaps of note that as part of the celebrations of George V's coronation, moving picture films of the actual coronation were brought to Dudley by Messrs Mahlers 'Belsize' Motor and exhibited at the public hall on the same evening.

Other national events were likewise marked locally, either with widespread celebrations, usually with church services, or memorial services, depending upon their nature, and with the town appropriately decorated. Such events include the relief of Ladysmith and Mafeking in 1900 and the ending of the Boer War in 1902. Probably the most internationally famous event of this period was the sinking of the liner RMS *Titanic* in 1912. Dudley had a special link with this ship, since her anchor, at the time the largest ever made, had been produced by N. Hingley & Sons of Netherton, and memorial services were held at various places of worship in the town following the disaster.

As well as Dudley's participation in national events, there was the tapestry of local, civic, political, commercial and industrial life. There were meetings of local organisations and events, local sporting events, and entertainments such as the Castle Fêtes, which were still being held yearly at Whitsun, the Dudley Horse Show, the Dudley Pageant in 1908, local theatrical and music hall productions and cinematic shows from about 1911, with shows at the Dudley Opera House and the opening of the New Empire Music Hall in 1903. There were elections in 1900, 1906 and 1910 (January and December) with the attendant campaigning. These were apparently events that engendered great interest.

The period also saw growth in new forms of transport. At the beginning of the century the use of the motor car was comparatively rare, and the preserve of the wealthy. Use grew until they, and the garages supplying them and related accessories, became much more commonplace. By 1913, though, only 512 vehicles had been registered in Dudley since registration began in 1903.

There were some civic improvements and developments during the period, for example, the new cemetery opening in 1903, the central library in 1909, and the geological museum, in the old library building in Priory Street/St James's Road, in 1912. The collection of fossils, said to be the second finest in the country, after those at the British Museum, was transferred there at the instigation of the corporation from the Mechanics Institute. Dudley also obtained a grant of a separate court of quarter sessions in 1908, the first sessions being held on 1 January 1909 at the Sessions Court, Priory Street. There were improvements in the field of education, such as the establishment of Dudley Education Committee in 1903, replacing the School Board, and the opening of the Upper Standard School in 1904. Dudley was also selected as one of the most suitable places in the country for the building of a teacher training college, to help to remedy the lack of such facilities. Dudley's college was opened in 1909, and in the following year Dudley Girls' High School opened in Priory Road.

In many ways, however, Dudley retained the appearance of a nineteenth-century town, with its old-established industries. Its slum housing remained, and calls had already begun for the corporation to step in and provide, or facilitate the building of, decent housing for the working population of the borough. This was to be one of the many changes brought about in the turbulent times which followed, but for Dudley, as for most of the country, the first years of the century were years of prosperity, growth, and stability.

Office staff, including the office boy, outside the premises of the Dudley Co-operative Bucket and Fender Company, Charlotte Street, *c.* 1900. The company was registered and commenced trading in 1888. It manufactured buckets, baths and other galvanised goods, and hearth furniture such as fenders, coal savers, and ash pans for the Co-operative Wholesale Society, and continued in business until the 1930s.

Fruit stall of R. Southall at Dudley Castle Fêtes, *c.* 1900. The stall bears the claim: 'This is the Noted Fruit Stall and Best Quality Only Sold from this Stall'. Goods for sale included pineapples, at 1*d* a slice, and bananas at 1*d* each. Richard Southall, English and foreign fruit salesman, claimed in his advertisements to be 'a dealer in all kinds of the choicest fruits when in season, finest and best fruits only in stock, orders attended to, flower shows, picnics etc. catered for'. He was caterer to the Dudley Castle Fêtes for many years, and attended Dudley, Brierley Hill and Wednesbury markets. Southall also had a shop at 44 Vauxhall Street.

Priory Street, *c.* 1900, looking from the corner of Wolverhampton Street from the former post office, towards the Saracen's Head, with the castle in the distance. On the left are 1 and 2 Priory Street, occupied by Hooper and Fairbairn, solicitors, and J. Shedden & Son, auctioneers, respectively. Next door is Dudley County Court, which was built and opened in 1858. Previously the court had been held at the town hall, also in Priory Street. On the right is the Crown Hotel with its splendid corner turret with windows. It was completed in 1898, and has recently been restored to its former glory.

Title page of the special spring issue of the new twentieth-century catalogue of Adshead & Smellie, Ivanhoe Fender and Grate Works, Oxford Street, Dudley, March 1900. The company manufactured fenders and hearth furniture at Ivanhoe Works, and items such as electric and gas fittings, table lamps and flower stands, jardinières, news racks and fire screens at the Collins Art Metal Works. The catalogue includes a special fireplace for the Paris Exhibition of 1900, from the designs by C.R. Ashbee of the Arts and Crafts Association. The firm claimed to be the largest manufacturers of artistic hearth suites in Great Britain.

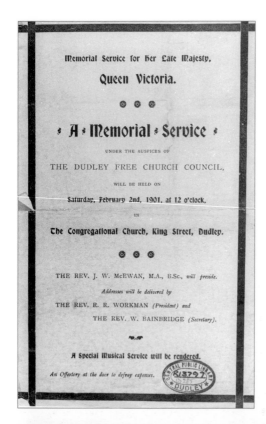

Order of service for a memorial service for the late Queen Victoria, held on Saturday 2 February 1901. Queen Victoria died on 22 January 1901 at Osborne House, Isle of Wight. The Prince of Wales was proclaimed king Edward VII on 24 January in London, and then in Dudley on 28 January. The queen's funeral took place on 2 February and memorial services, held nationally at all places of worship, drew large congregations. During the time of the funeral, businesses were closed, and flags were flown at half mast. This service, at King Street Congregational church, under the auspices of the Dudley Free Church Council, was presided over by the Rev. J. W. McEwan, the minister at the church.

The cast of Dudley Amateur Operatic Society in their production of Gilbert and Sullivan's *The Mikado*, performed at Dudley Opera House for one week from 27 May 1901. The Operatic Society was revived and put on a business footing in 1898. Their first production was *HMS Pinafore* in 1899. This was followed by *The Yeomen of the Guard* and *Iolanthe*, with the honorary conductor and stage manager Mr J. Randall Cooke, and secretary Mr H. Preedy. The players in *The Mikado* were as follows: The Mikado: Mr I. Fellows; Nanki Poo: Mr H.L. Cox; Ko-Ko: Mr Hastings-Grainger; Poo-Bah: Mr J. Reidy; Pish-Tash: Mr S. Harvey; Yum-Yum: Miss L. Yeomans; Pitti-Sing: Miss Gertrude Betts; Peep-Bo: Miss Rose Gee; and Katesha: Miss Bird.

Wolverhampton Street, 1902, with placards outside the *Herald* office and printing works, no. 210, proclaiming peace and the end of the Boer War. The war ended on 31 May 1902, and news arrived in Dudley during the evening of 1 June. On 2 June every house and place of business was decorated with flags. In the evening a special service of thanksgiving was held at the parish church, attended by a large congregation, including the mayor and some of the corporation who marched to the church, led by the Dudley Town Brass Band. On 3 June there was a torchlight procession, followed by fireworks. Thanksgiving services were held on 8 June throughout the country by command of the King.

Dudley Horse Show at Priory Fields, Monday and Tuesday 1 and 2 August 1904. On the Monday various competitions, including pony races, were held. On Tuesday there was a horse show, and the new features of push ball competitions and an airship ascent, billed as 'probably never again to be witnessed in the Midlands', attracted a great deal of attention. There were also fireworks by James Pain & Son of London. The horse show seems to have developed from the Dudley Cycle and Trades Parade held from about 1894. The first horse show, and ninth cycle parade, was held in August 1902, and the horse show was then held annually until at least 1909, when the cycle parade was held again.

Entrance to the new cemetery at Springsmire, Stourbridge Road, 1904. The new cemetery was opened by the Mayor on 30 September 1903. The vicar of Dudley, the vicar of St Luke's and other clergy, as well as aldermen and councillors, the town clerk and his deputy, and the borough surveyor were also present. After the purchase of the land the surveyor, Mr Gammage, was instructed to prepare plans for laying out the ground, two cemetery chapels, registrar's lodge and offices. Contracts were given to several different firms, including the Dudley Art Metal Company for the fencing, and Mark Round for the chapel and lodge. After the opening ceremony prayers were offered in the chapel.

Artist's impression of the soldiers' memorial for fallen heroes in the Boer War, 1899–1902, taken from the *Dudley Herald*'s souvenir of its unveiling at the Borough Cemetery on 23 September 1904. This memorial to the fifty-six Dudley men who died cost about £300 and was financed by public subscription. The sculptor was Henry Owen Burgess of Old Hill. The memorial was unveiled by Lt Gen Sir Nevill Gerald Lyttleton, and the mayor and corporation and the memorial committee assembled at the Town Hall to receive him and the other guests. The party included survivors of the war, wearing medals and clasps, who processed to the cemetery for the ceremony.

Officers of the Dudley division of the St John Ambulance Brigade outside their headquarters in Stone Street, 1905. The division was formed in 1892 and is said to be the oldest in the Midlands and the second oldest in the country. Standing in the centre is Sgt Charles Ollis. He was associated with the brigade for more than forty-five years, joining in 1895 and retiring in 1933; he died in 1941. The other officers are not named but the corps superintendent, W.E. Hartland, is probably seated in the centre. He was one of the first members of the Dudley corps and superintendent from 1904 to 1919. Others present could be Sgt E.B. Griffin, Sergeant Alexander (Round Oak section), Sgt Maud (Stourbridge section), and Cpl Tibbetts, the honorary treasurer.

Dudley Conservative Club, winners of the Birmingham Suburban Conservative Clubs' Billiards League challenge cup, 1905/6. Back row, left to right: John Davis, Frank Deeley, T.F.W. Higgs, H.W. Hughes (captain). Seated: Hugh Smith, W.H. Thompson, A.E. Marston (deputy captain), J. Bullock. Dudley Conservative Club, Castle Hill, was inaugurated on 24 March and opened on 14 October 1884. There were dining, smoking, reading and card rooms, a fully equipped billiard room, with two tables by Burroughs and Watts, and a bowling green and skittle alley at the Trindle. In 1906 membership was about 250 and there had been more than 11,000 visitors to the club since its opening. The club closed in 1975 and was redeveloped as an office.

Advertisement from Blocksidge's *Dudley Almanack*, 1906, for Mr and Mrs Robert Barlow, 57 King Street. Mrs Barlow is shown in her academic gown as a teacher of the piano, violin, mandolin and all stringed instruments. Mr Barlow was a pianoforte tuner and repairer, and dealer in pianos, organs and all musical instruments. They were also dealers in perfumery. The Barlows were in business and advertising by 1902 and continued advertising until 1910. From 1911 Mrs Barlow only is listed (as a teacher of music), and it is likely that Mr Barlow had died. She continued at the address until at least 1923.

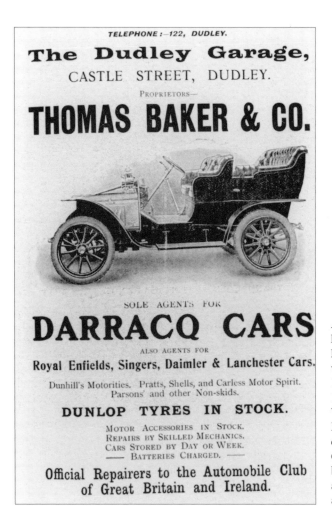

Advertisement from Blocksidge's *Dudley Almanack*, 1907, for Dudley Garage, Castle Street, whose proprietors were Thomas Baker and Co. They were sole agents for Darracq cars, which were of French origin and developed between 1891 and 1896. The firm seems to have been established in about 1905, later becoming Dudley Garage Motor Co. and then Westley's Dudley Garage Ltd. The firm also supplied Dunhill's Motorities, which were motorists' protective clothing, especially ladies' boots and veils; and Pratt's, Shells and Carless Motor Spirit, fuel which was sold in 2-gallon cans before the advent of petrol pumps. In 1912 the firm advertised that it supplied aeroplanes, motor clothing and accessories, and sold cars on deferred payment.

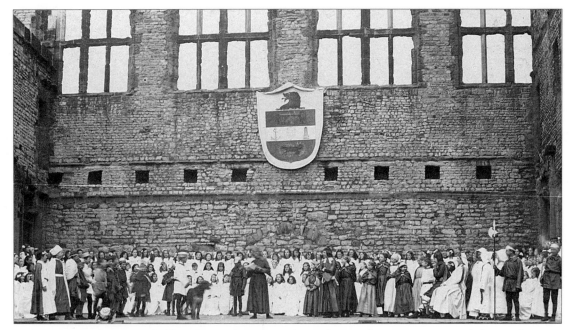

Dudley Historical Pageant, held in the castle courtyard at Whitsuntide, 1908, as part of the Castle Fêtes. There were eight episodes illustrating the history of Dudley and its castle and priory, from the foundation of Dudley Castle to the petition of Dud Dudley to Charles II in 1660 for the revival of his patent for making iron with pit coal. This photograph apparently shows episode six, dealing with the quarrel between Lord Dudley and William de Bermingham, de Bermingham's defiance and the reconciliation of both parties. Children from various schools took part: those in episode six were from Wolverhampton Street and Park Schools. Roger de Somery was played by Master Knight, and William de Bermingham by Master Roberts.

The four elder children of the Rt Hon. Earl of Dudley, 1909. Left to right: Lady Morvyth Lilian Ward, -?-, Hon. Lady Gladys Honour Ward and William Humble Eric Ward, Viscount Ednam, later third Earl of Dudley. The child in the sailor suit, in front, is the Hon. Roderick John Ward. This photograph was included in Blocksidge's *Dudley Almanack*, 1909, to mark the earl's visit to the town on 10 June 1908. He attended a banquet held in his honour at the Dudley Arms hotel, and went on to the castle to watch the pageant. Soon after, he left the country for Australia to take up his new post as Governor General.

Opening of the new Dudley Training College by the Rt Hon Walter Runciman MP, minister of education, 16 July 1909. The Board of Education had identified a lack of teacher training places, and in order to remedy this encouraged the erection of national training colleges. Dudley was selected as a suitable place. The foundation stone for the building was laid on 10 September 1908 by the Countess of Dudley. The building was designed by Crouch, Butler and Savage, architects of Birmingham, and erected by Oakely and Coulson of Dudley. The college was successful and, with a large demand for places, it was extended to accommodate more students soon after its opening.

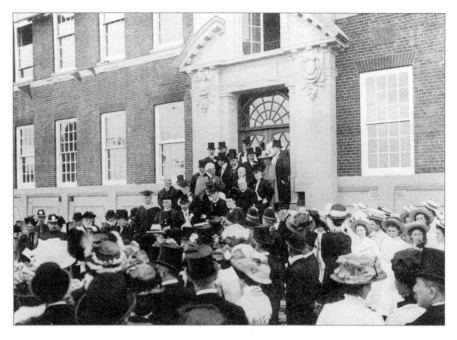

Newly appointed principal and staff of the new Dudley Training College outside the entrance to the college, 1909. Ivor B. Johns MA, Goldsmith's College, late Senior Fellow of the University of Wales (seated), was principal until 1913. The vice-principal, Miss C.J.M. Hubbard, formerly head of the Chester City and County Girls' School, is on his right. Also present are F.W. Wynne, secretary; Mr W.J. Lewis, BSc, assistant secretary; Mr W.T. Holme BA; Miss E.G. Hearn BSc (middle at back); Mr R. Townsend MSc; and Miss M.M. Holliday (left front). This photograph was reproduced by permission of Britten and Hill, Dudley, from whom it could be obtained in picture postcard form for 1*d.*

Staff preparing to open the new central library, St James's Road, 1909. It is likely that these are Miss E.J. Southall, chief librarian, and one of her sisters, Miss E.L. or Miss A.R. Southall, both assistant librarians. Their father William Southall had been appointed librarian in 1888 and was assisted by his daughters. The new building, which replaced the library opened in 1884, included a reference library, magazine room and lending department. It provided research rooms, including a separate ladies' reading room on the first floor, but only library staff had direct access to books on the shelves. Even lending books were requested and then delivered to borrowers in the central hall. Open access in the lending library was not adopted until 1933.

Erecting the statue on the top of the new central library, 1909. This was described as of 'heroic size' and symbolises philosophy, while the statues over the public entrance represented science and literature. In this picture are, from the left: Alderman F.W. Cook JP, member of the public libraries committee, Mr Round, Mr Wenyon and another Mr Round. Mr George H. Wenyon was the architect and Messrs Mark Round and Sons were the contractors for the building. The library was opened by the Hon John Herbert Ward, accompanied by his wife, on 16 September 1909. A grant of £7,500 from Andrew Carnegie made the building possible.

Old Woolpack, Castle Street, opposite New Street, *c.* 1910. The gentleman outside the front entrance is probably Arthur Gillman, licensee from 1910 to 1913. The Old Woolpack was one of the oldest public houses in Dudley. It was established in 1622 and demolished as part of the Hall Street redevelopment in 1966. The election posters 'Vote for Boscawen' and 'Tariff Reform' suggest a date of 1910. Sir Arthur Griffith Boscawen stood as a Unionist candidate for Dudley in both the January and December elections of 1910, on a platform of tariff reform. In the January election he was defeated by the Liberal candidate, A.G. Hooper (MP for Dudley 1906–10). In December, however, Boscawen was elected with a majority of 360. He continued to serve as MP until 1921.

Netherton St Andrew's football team and club officials, outside the club house at Netherton Cricket Club, with St Andrew's church in the background, 1910. In the *Dudley Herald* there are reports of games played by the team in October and November, including home fixtures played at the Dingle. These include St Andrew's Past *v.* Present on 22 October. Members of the Present team were: Poole, Knott, Hill, the Rev. H.C.B. Roden (captain, and curate of St Andrew's), Hudson, F. Round, Kilvert, Homer, Downs, and F. Keeling. The Past team consisted of: Deeley, Spencer, F. Hilbanks, W. Gilbanks, J. Round (captain), J. Boote, Woodhall, Flavell, H. Hill, Hudson, and Cooksey. At the final whistle Present had won 4–2.

Public proclamation of George V as king at the town hall, Priory Street, 10 May 1910, by the mayor, Councillor J.A. Hillman, accompanied by his chaplain and the town clerk. The ceremony was repeated in Dudley Market Place and at Netherton and Woodside. Edward VII had died on 6 May. The mayor had wired the Home Secretary an expression of the town's sympathy, flags were at half mast, blinds were drawn, sports cancelled, and in the evening muffled peals were rung at the parish church and theatres and cinemas were closed. The following day the vicar of Dudley paid tribute to the late king at the parish church where the pulpit and lectern were draped with the royal colours.

St Thomas's church, Dudley, decorated in memory of the late Edward VII, probably for the public memorial service held there on 20 May, the day of the king's funeral. The mayor led a procession to the church. The church was decorated with the royal emblems of woe, purple and white in front of the pulpit and a crown of white flowers, with the letters ER in a floral design, in front of the altar. The parishioners had also sent a wreath to Windsor in the form of ER with a harp between, bearing the message 'from the Parish Church, Dudley, God Rest the King'.

Sir Gilbert Claughton, with his Airedale terrier, Jack, *c.* 1911.
Sir Gilbert's association with Dudley began in 1884 when he
took up an appointment at Castle Mill Works. He became
manager of the Earl of Dudley's collieries and in 1887 took over
the management of the Earl's Himley estates, and coal and iron
interests. He was also chairman of the LNWR and a director of
Round Oak Steel Works. He served as mayor four times in
succession, 1891–94, and became a freeman of the Borough of
Dudley, and a baronet, in 1912. He stood for Parliament in
1906 as the Unionist candidate, being narrowly defeated by the
Liberal, Mr A.G. Hooper. Sir Gilbert died on 28 June 1921, aged
sixty-five.

Postcard view of Dudley Market Place, decorated for the coronation of George V, 22 June 1911. Local celebrations included
dinners for poor people aged sixty-five and above; a tea for all schoolchildren under fifteen; commemoration medals for
schoolchildren; and bands playing in the various recreation grounds, the Market Place and the castle courtyard. The council
decided not to spend any money on decorations, fireworks or illuminations but the mayor asked the shopkeepers and inhabitants
to decorate their premises for the event. This was done especially in High Street, Wolverhampton Street and the Market Place.
A commemoration service was held at St Thomas's, which was decorated for the occasion, and at other places of worship.

Local companies of the Territorial Army on parade in Castle Street, passing the junction with Fisher Street, 30 July 1911. The parade was headed by the band of the Worcestershire Hussars. A church parade such as this was the practice on the last Sunday before the annual training camp, which in 1911 was held for fourteen days at Conway. The local territorial force was made up of G and H companies of the 7th Battalion Worcestershire Regiment. G Company was under the command of Capt Thompson and H under that of O.S. Hooper. These companies replaced the first Volunteer Battalion of the Worcestershire Regiment under the Territorial and Reserve Forces Act in 1908 to form the nucleus of a new citizen's army.

Exterior and interior views of the premises of William Cranage, 69 High Street, which appeared in the publication *The Commercial, Residential and Educational Facilities of Dudley and District: The Official Handbook*, issued under the authority of Dudley Corporation and the chamber of commerce, 1912. This is described as an up-to-date confectionery business and is advertised in Blocksidge's *Dudley Almanack* for 1913 as having a new café serving afternoon teas in a cosy tea room and specialising in all sizes of rich quality wedding cakes, beautifully decorated. A selection of these products can be seen both in the windows and on the counters with signs advertising ices. The business seems to have been established at 69 High Street by 1910, trading first as A. Cranage and then as F.A. Cranage and from 1912 as William Cranage. It seems to have expanded quite soon and in Blocksidge's *Almanack* for 1914 the firm is advertising home-made chocolates, made on the premises in over fifty varieties. A 1 lb box could be sent, postage free, to any address, for *2s 6d*.

Grange Park from Himley Road, also taken from the corporation and chamber of commerce *Official Handbook*, 1912. This park was formed from land purchased by the corporation from the trustees of Dudley Blue Coat School in 1891, and was laid out as a recreation ground between 1892 and 1893, under the direction of the borough surveyor, John Gammage. The scheme was intended to provide employment during the winter months, as advised by the Local Government Board. The work of levelling and laying out the park apparently continued during 1893. It seems possible that this had been completed by January 1894, when this and Buffery Park were inspected by the council's estates committee. No details of any official opening have been found, however.

Alexandra Day flower sellers, 28 June 1913. Seventy ladies, dressed in white with pink and white sashes and wearing wreaths of roses, sold artificial white roses in the street in honour of Queen Alexandra, and to raise funds for local charities. Local tradesmen showed their patriotic appreciation with a liberal display of flags and bunting. F.W. Cook's attracted particular attention, with its exterior decorations and twenty of its windows arranged with flowers. The headquarters was a room at the Temperance Institute, and the chairman and secretary were Mrs W.H. Thompson of Dudley and Mrs Arthur Bird, respectively. The district raised £217 in total, from which the Guest Hospital benefited. Dudley alone raised £100.

2. The First World War: 1914–1918

This large crowd is gathered in the Market Place for a special service for Dudley's reservists and terriers on 5 August 1915. The two Dudley companies of territorials of the 7th Battalion Worcestershire Regiment, G Company, under Capt Thompson and H Company under Capt Adams, were called up on the first day of the war and departed the following day. The mayor spoke from an improvised platform and wished the men 'God Speed' and the vicar offered prayers for their safe return. The men then marched away down High Street with the cheers of their relatives and friends ringing in their ears.

Introduction

When war broke out in Europe in the summer of 1914 it was hardly unexpected. Tensions had been obvious in Europe for a decade, and war was seen as inevitable. Even the name the Great War had already been coined long before the conflict actually broke out. For Britain the war began on Tuesday 4 August, after a Bank Holiday weekend. The following day all military and naval reservists and territorials were called up, and the Defence of the Realm Act passed later in the month gave the government wide-ranging powers to requisition land and property, and bring the railways and docks under its control. This was to be Britain's first experience of total war.

Lord Kitchener appealed for one million new recruits, and there was no shortage of volunteers in the early days of the war. Very few guessed, though, just how long the conflict would last. Even Field Marshal Sir John French, commander of the British Expeditionary Forces, apparently thought that the war would be over by Christmas.

The BEF, comprising about seventy thousand regular troops and reservists, landed in France on 17 August. The 2nd and 3rd Worcesters, which included several Dudley men, were with them. Their first engagement was on the Belgian frontier at Mons, where the British suffered heavy casualties, and were forced to begin retreating on 23 August.

Meanwhile, at home, Dudley gave its reservists and terriers a big send off on 5 August. The *Dudley Herald* described the scene at the station, where many women saw off their menfolk, some in tears but others 'like true English women . . . bore up bravely during the actual moments of parting in order that the men should not be discouraged at the thought of weeping women left behind'. On 6 October 300 men of the new Worcestershire (Reserve) Battalion left for Kidderminster, on their way to the front. There was no official announcement of any kind, but still tradesmen had put out flags and thousands of people, on hearing the bands, turned out in Market Place to wish them well.

At home, the first impact of the war was a rise in prices brought on by panic buying, and a reduction in trade. Many people were put out of work as a result and in October 1914 Dudley's mayoress and the local branch of the Work for Women Fund held a flag day to raise money to find useful work for recently unemployed women. Before long, however, the war had created a great many more jobs for women, including some which had previously been reserved for men. In Dudley many women were needed in the factories, in particular those making munitions, such as Messrs Harper Sons & Bean, and from 1916 the National Projectile Factory. Women also played a role in caring for wounded soldiers, as nurses and members of the VAD (Voluntary Aid Detachments), both at home, in hospitals such as the Guest in Dudley, and overseas. The first Dudley Roll of Honour, published in the *Dudley Herald* on 24 October 1914, giving the names, addresses and regiments of local men serving in the forces, also included a section of 'Ladies at the Front'.

The upheaval which the war caused in Britain was as nothing compared to the situation in Belgium, where thousands of people fled the advancing German army. In the first two months of the war around six thousand Belgians arrived in Britain, and the numbers continued to grow. In early October 1914, at a public meeting in Dudley Town Hall, it was agreed that the town would accommodate some refugees. The first twenty-two arrived on 21 October, and were followed by another batch in November, who were accommodated at Wellfield House. In early 1915 a hostel for refugees was established in Castle Street, but there was friction there between French and Flemish speaking Belgians, so a second hostel was provided in Old Cross Street, for the Flemish speakers. The people of Dudley were generous in providing supplies for their new neighbours, and local tradesmen provided bread and groceries, while money was also raised for them.

Fund-raising events, such as concerts and collections, were commonplace during the war. On a local level, besides the Belgian refugees, money was raised for the Red Cross, St John Ambulance, local prisoners of war, soldiers' dependants, returned soldiers and so on. Nationally the government organised 'Tank Weeks' and 'Feed the Guns Weeks' as well as advertising the sale of war bonds.

The Armistice of 11 November 1918 was greeted, as expected, with great celebration everywhere, and Dudley was no exception. The joy and relief, however, was tempered by concern for those still in the forces, and sorrow for the fallen. At the outbreak of war Britain's standing army totalled 160,000 men; within a year three million were in uniform, and by the end of the war twenty-three million. The public demanded speedy demobilisation, and by November 1920 the number of servicemen was reduced to 370,000. Sick and wounded soldiers continued to arrive back home well into 1919, and the VADs were not demobilised until late that year. It is estimated that one in ten British men were lost in the First World War, and a further half a million were seriously wounded. Dudley alone lost around six hundred men. The Treaty of Versailles, signed in June 1919, demanded huge compensation from Germany. Lloyd George considered the terms of the finished document so harsh that 'we shall have to fight another war all over again in twenty-five years at three times the cost'. The seeds of the Second World War had already been sown.

BANK HOLIDAY EXTENDED.

BY ORDER OF THE GOVERNMENT

Till FRIDAY, 7th of AUGUST, 1914, all Banks will be closed throughout Great Britain and Ireland.

Notice of extension of the August Bank Holiday, 1914. On 4 August 1914 Great Britain declared war on Germany and the armed forces were mobilised. Notices like this one soon appeared on banks and public buildings, and became the focus of much popular interest. The declaration of war had an immediate impact for many Dudley residents. Trade fell off sharply, so that many people were either put out of work, or on short time. There was also panic buying of groceries and, in consequence, prices rose quickly in the first weeks of the war. Several shops closed or reduced their opening hours. Government reassurances of ample food supplies soon calmed the situation.

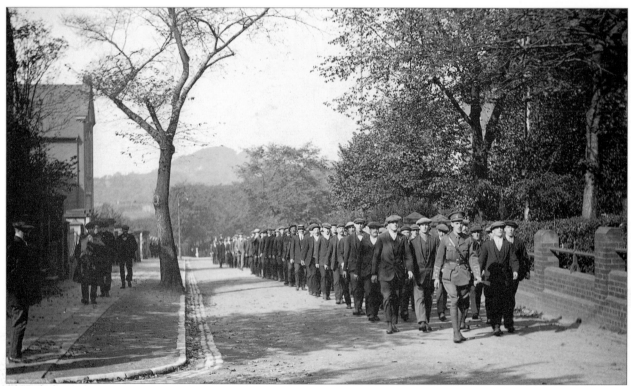

A group of volunteers march along Priory Road, *c.* 1914. Dudley had some initial problems with recruitment when its permanent recruiting officers were called up for duty elsewhere but a Sgt Maj Chiverton was appointed as replacement and turned the town hall into a recruiting office. Chiverton was a career soldier, who had seen action with the 87th Royal Irish Fusiliers. He was transferred to the 1st Volunteer Battalion Worcestershire Regiment in 1883, and discharged from the Army in 1903, because of his age. Chiverton came in for some criticism for rejecting large numbers of recruits, but by early December he had enlisted 1,097 men for Kitchener's Army and a further 350 for the 7th Reserve Battalion Worcestershire Regiment.

Requisitioning of horses for use by troops, in Netherton, August 1914. Almost immediately after the war began, a large number of horses were commandeered by the army. The authorities promised that, wherever possible, no horse would be taken which was involved in trade, but nevertheless some were, and many firms had to curtail their transport as a result. A great deal of inconvenience was caused in many quarters by the sudden loss of horses. On Wednesday 5 and Thursday 6 August, horses which had been commandeered in Dudley and Netherton were paraded in King Street, before Capt R.L.Green MRCVS, and Mr A. Green MRCVS, and examined before going to the front under an escort of a squad of the Wiltshire Regiment. All the best light and draught horses were taken. Sixty-five were entrained in the first two days of the war, and the total number taken from the district eventually reached around two hundred.

An advertisement for F.W. Cook, Ltd, published in Blocksidge's *Dudley Almanack*, 1914. Frederick William Cook was a member of Dudley Town Council continually from 1897 until his death in 1938, served two consecutive terms as mayor, from November 1906, and was elected an alderman in 1908. He was a firm believer in the power of advertising and advertisements for the shop appear regularly in the local press throughout the war. Cook was clearly concerned about the effect on trade, and in several editions in the early months of the war exhorts the public to continue buying as usual 'to prevent unemployment and assist the general welfare of the nation at this critical period'.

Dudley Junior Conservative Club new premises, 1914. The club's home in Tower Street had been recognised as inadequate for several years, but purchase and extension had been ruled impractical. In 1911 the chairman announced that negotiations were under way to buy Priory House. Before the new Junior Conservative Club opened there a three-storey extension was added and the existing building was refurbished. The new premises then included a bowling alley, billiard room, assembly hall for meetings and dances, which was lacking in Tower Street; a smoke room and bar, card room, dining room, committee room and rooms for the caretaker. The Conservative and Unionist Association is still based there today.

Recruiting advertisement from the *Dudley Herald*, January 1915. Much social pressure was exerted on men to join up, and many who did not found themselves presented with white feathers in the street. Regular adverts appealing for recruits were published in the local press, and employers were urged to persuade their young male employees to enlist – some men were even sacked if they refused. Still, in Dudley, a patriotic meeting held in November 1914 resulted in no new recruits. It had become all too obvious that volunteers could not meet the army's needs, so the government began moving towards conscription.

St John Ambulance Brigade, Netherton division, flag day, 28 August 1915. This event raised around £17 for the branch's funds, which had been depleted by war work. The Netherton branch formed part of the Dudley and District Corps which by this date had provided seventy-six ambulance men for service overseas and at war hospitals across Britain. Most of those members left behind had also volunteered and were awaiting orders. Meanwhile, they continued to do valuable work at home, offering first aid in the street, at factory accidents and in cases of sudden illness. On the flag day itself, three members of the brigade administered first aid to PC Large, who had his jaw broken by a drunken man.

A group of Belgian refugees at Dibdale House, Dudley, 1914. At a public meeting at Dudley Town Hall on 29 September it was agreed that Dudley should join forces with Birmingham to accommodate a number of refugees. The first group of 22 Belgians (pictured) arrived on 21 October and were put up at Dibdale House, which had been lent free of charge by Mr Newey. Most of these refugees came from Aerschot, between Malines and Diest, with the exception of the two nuns who came from Malines, and had seen their convent burnt down. All had a story to tell, and at least two of the men claimed to have been captured by the Germans and escaped.

Dudley Patriotic Committee, 1916. The committee was formed at the outbreak of war to raise money for war charities such as the Belgian Refugees Fund and the Guest Hospital, and to send comforts to the troops. Regular parcels of food were sent to all Dudley prisoners of war and to local men at the front, and in 1915 the committee even sent 100 mouth organs to the Worcesters in France. As the war went on, and the number of Dudley men in uniform and in POW camps increased, the Patriotic Committee found its resources severely stretched and urged every employee in Dudley to give a penny a week for the fund. The appeals continued until the end of the war.

The 1st Battalion Worcestershire Volunteer Regiment, above on parade in 1916, and below, an undated photograph of Dudley Company machine gun section on manoeuvres. The Volunteer Regiment was made up of men whose age, fitness or duties at home prevented them joining the regulars. Similar groups sprang up across the country from the outbreak of war, and old soldiers were found to drill them. In Dudley, eighty men attended the first drill of the Volunteer Training Corps, in 1914, with Sgt Maj Chiverton as instructor, and Capt Mold, a master at the grammar school and ex-officer with the territorials, in command. The War Office granted official recognition to these groups after a few months and provided each man with a red arm band. No other government funding was provided. In Dudley the members paid 10s each per year for administration and provided their own uniforms. Other equipment was paid for by voluntary subscription. By July 1915 £229 16s had been raised, but it was estimated that a further £250 would be needed to provide every man with a rifle and full kit. Also in 1915 the Dudley Company established a drum and bugle band (which became the battalion band), a motorcycle corps and signalling section.

COUNTY BOROUGH OF DUDLEY.

LIGHTING RESTRICTIONS.

The Watch Committee of the Dudley Town Council have decided to put in force the following Lighting Restrictions and householders, manufacturers, tradesmen and others are asked to loyally co-operate in carrying the Restrictions into effect at once :---

(1) All Lights outside buildings to be kept unlit and all lights inside houses, works, shops, factories, etc., and all roof lights to be effectually shaded.

(2) No strong head lights or search-lights to be used on motor cars or other vehicles.

(3) No lights of any description to be used in the open market, and every stall holder to comply promptly with any requirements of the police as to lights in the market.

(4) All Illuminated Clocks to be darkened.

(5) The drivers of Motor Cars and other vehicles shall immediately pull up on being requested or signalled to do so by any Constable.

4th February, 1916.

S. C. LLOYD,
MAYOR.

Blocksidge, Printer, Dudley.

A poster outlining lighting restrictions, 4 February 1916. Just five days previously Dudley, and other parts of the Black Country, had been bombed by a Zeppelin. No-one was killed but a great deal of damage was done. An earlier raid on other parts of the Midlands had resulted in 67 deaths and 117 injuries. However, not everyone was in favour of lighting restrictions. Some argued that they were unnecessary and positively dangerous, and that the black out would never be total, since furnaces would still glow and tram wires flash. Alderman Cook, owner of F.W. Cook's store, argued in a town council meeting that the restrictions were having a detrimental effect on shopkeepers; as soon as the lights were dimmed, the town emptied.

COUNTY BOROUGH OF DUDLEY.

WARNING OF ENEMY AIRCRAFT.

At my request the Dudley Company of the Worcestershire Volunteer Regiment have agreed to assist in giving Warning of the approach of Enemy Aircraft.

Patrols will be posted nightly in and around Dudley, and will give warning by firing 3 rifle shots in rapid succession.

On this warning being given the precautions as issued by Superintendent Speke should be rigidly observed.

It is proposed on Sunday Afternoon next, February 13th, between 3 and 4 o'clock, to test the efficiency of these signals.

S. C. LLOYD,
MAYOR.

Town Hall, Dudley,
February 8th, 1916.

Blooksidge, Printer, Dudley.

A poster warning of enemy aircraft, 8 February 1916. These provisions too are clearly a result of January's Zeppelin raid. Debate continued, however, about air raid warnings throughout the war. The Dudley police and some members of the town council disagreed with audible warnings, arguing that it led to panic and caused people to rush into the streets. Some workers, however, threatened to strike in May 1916 if the town council decided not to sound a hooter. In October the council decided against a sound warning of an air raid, although the position was somewhat ridiculous – since neighbouring boroughs sounded hooters that could be heard by many Dudley residents.

Workers at the National Projectile Factory, Dudley, *c.* 1916. This was a purpose built munitions factory. The Ministry of Munitions authorised construction in August 1915, and the buildings were completed the following May. Until September 1916, however, all forging was done by other firms, since the partly built forging shop was blown down in a gale at Christmas 1915. The factory began by producing 6 in shells and 60 lb shrapnel shells, but received orders from the Admiralty in 1917 for 6 in chemical shells. This eventually overtook production of the high explosive shells. A steel shortage in early 1918 reduced shrapnel production, and in March the shrapnel plant became an aero-engine works, but the National Projectile Factory continued to make shells until the end of 1918.

Making 60 lb shrapnel shells at the National Projectile Factory. The new factory originally employed around four thousand workers. Here, as elsewhere, many of them were women (munitionettes) and youths. In late 1916 the government began appealing for 'women of leisure' to do their bit for the war effort by volunteering for munitions work. Free training classes were offered to them, giving six weeks instruction in the basics of bench and vice work, turning, milling and drilling. After training, the ladies had to go to a factory and be willing to work the same hours as the other women for the same pay. Working hours varied, although fifty-three hours per week was about average, but pay was generally very good. The work could be dangerous, though, and the chemicals used often turned the skin yellow.

N.P.F. Dudley.
acing Base End of
0 pdr. Shrapnel Shell

A young boy working on a 60 lb shrapnel shell, National Projectile Factory, *c.* 1916. The factory was run by Messrs Harper, Sons and Bean, who had been making munitions in their own factory since the outbreak of war but were unable to meet demand. More than five thousand people were already engaged in munitions work in Dudley in 1915 and the influx of munitions workers for the new factory made Dudley's existing housing problem more acute. The Town Council acquired land at Brewery Fields and, in conjunction with the Ministry of Munitions, built houses and hostels there. These hutments were built of wood on concrete and brick foundations. The cottages had either two or three bedrooms, while the hostels consisted of communal rooms and several small cubicles for sleeping. When they were built they were considered better than many permanent working class houses in the town, but they soon proved to be a fire hazard and later became insanitary. The hutments were ceremoniously fired in 1933.

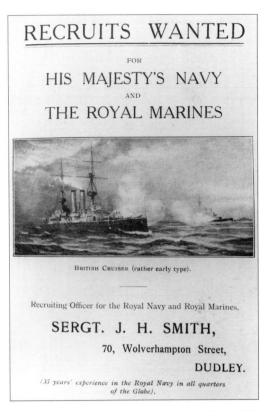

This recruiting advertisement for the Navy and Royal Marines appeared in Blocksidge's *Dudley Almanack* for 1916. The First World War is mostly associated with trench warfare, and in fact there was only one major naval battle, at Jutland in May 1916, but the Navy was involved in several other skirmishes, as well as protecting British merchant shipping convoys, and troops landing at Gallipoli. Most of the men who volunteered for service in Dudley joined the Worcestershire Regiment, but some did join the Navy or Marines. Of around six hundred men listed in Dudley's Roll of Honour for the First World War, only sixteen were enlisted in the 'senior service'.

A YMCA hut, pictured in Blocksidge's *Dudley Almanack* for 1916. This hut is probably not in Dudley, but the Dudley branch of the Young Men's Christian Association was active during the war, raising money to provide huts and tents with recreational facilities for local soldiers in training elsewhere in Britain, and at the front. At the outbreak of war members of the Dudley YMCA volunteered to work at Whittington Barracks, Lichfield, where they erected a tent and organised entertainment for the troops. Among the volunteers were the Dudley branch secretary, T.K. Banks, and one James Whale, a Dudleian by birth but later a famous Hollywood film director, and recently the subject of the award winning film *Gods and Monsters*.

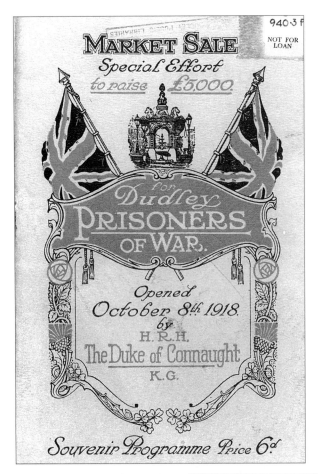

Market Sale souvenir programme, October 1918. The Market Sale was organised by the Dudley Patriotic Committee to raise £5,000 for its work. It ran from 8 to 12 October in Market Place, over which a huge tent had been erected. Inside were various stalls, organised by local churches, committees and organisations such as the Licensed Victuallers Association. The opening ceremony on the first day was performed by HRH the Duke of Connaught, the first royal visitor to Dudley since Elizabeth I. The local theatres and the Trindle Road skating rink held special shows, and gave profits to the fund. Altogether the Market Sale week raised over £11,000.

Feed the Guns campaign, Dudley Market Place, November 1918. This was part of a national campaign to raise money for the war effort. On 2 November the guns arrived at the borough boundary where a procession was formed, led by the band of the 1st Worcestershire Volunteer Regiment and including cadets, discharged soldiers and munitions workers. The guns stayed in Market Place for one week, during which soldiers put on displays of camouflage techniques, signalling and gas attacks. The post office set up a 'big gun hut' to meet the demand for government bonds. Nationally the government had appealed for £1,000 million to continue the war. Dudley's final total was £500,000.

Dudley decorated for the Armistice, November 1918: above, Market Place, and right, the Worcestershire Furnishing Company in Wolverhampton Street. News of the peace reached Dudley at around 10.30 a.m. on Monday 11 November 1918. Before the newspapers made the announcement factory bells and buzzers were sounded, workers left the factories and the streets became crowded. Bunting soon appeared in the streets, and the crowds acquired rosettes and other emblems with the national colours. Amongst all the joy, however, the mayor sounded a note of restraint, by remembering the sorrow of thousands who had lost loved ones in the conflict. On Monday evening a procession set out from Waddam's Pool with banners, flags and torches. It was made up of several hundred people and four bands. There was a strong police presence in the town, but the night passed off peacefully with no arrests. The wartime rules on sales of fireworks were immediately relaxed and a display was put on in the castle grounds. The celebrations went on well into the night, although many pubs had closed in the early evening when they ran out of supplies! The celebrations continued into Tuesday and Wednesday, with many works closing down, and the streets remaining thronged with revellers. Meanwhile, church services of thanksgiving and remembrance were held across the borough.

COUNTY BOROUGH OF DUDLEY

DUDLEY MARKETS

NOTICE IS HEREBY GIVEN
that the Dudley Markets will be

CLOSED
ON PEACE DAY,

Saturday, the 19th July, instant, but
will be open on FRIDAY, the 18th
instant.

TOWN HALL,
DUDLEY.   **ARTHUR HOLT,**
4th July, 1919.   TOWN CLERK.

HERALD PRESS, DUDLEY.

Peace Day, July 1919: left, a poster giving
notice of the closure of Dudley markets for
the occasion on Saturday 19 July, and above,
a procession in Netherton. Although the end
of the First World War is always associated
with Armistice Day, 11 November 1918, the
peace was not official until the signing of the
Treaty of Versailles on 28 June 1919. In
Dudley, as in the rest of Britain, the news
was a cause for further celebration. A
procession of soldiers, sailors and airmen
was organised in Dudley for 5 August. Over
3,000 returned servicemen were present to
be welcomed home by the townspeople. The
celebrations on Peace Day itself, 17 July, were
mainly for the local children, and the streets
were once again decorated.

3. Between the Wars

Aerial photograph of Dudley, by Aerofilms Ltd, 12 September 1924. This is a view of Dudley from the south. Stafford Street is on the right, with St Thomas's church at the top, and the gasometer and works of the Dudley Gas Light Company in Spring Gardens on the right. Wolverhampton Street is shown from its junction with Stafford Street in the direction of the centre of the town. Southalls Lane and Cross Street can be seen, with Wolverhampton Street Schools and the Presbyterian church, with spire, on the left, and Wolverhampton Street Methodist church, The Inhedge, Lloyd's Bank and Horseley House and Gardens on the right. The area is built up with houses and factories and before any modern developments.

Introduction

The 1920s were a time of general frivolity, with the 'flappers' and 'bright young things' making the most of peace after the horrors of the Great War, but the inter-war years are mainly remembered for the Great Depression, which afflicted much of the world after 1929.

At the beginning of the period Dudley was largely as it had been at the beginning of the century, but the ensuing years saw many changes and developments. The 1920s did not bring the return to settled prosperity that millions had hoped for after the end of the First World War and the promise given to returning servicemen of 'a land fit for returning heroes to live in' was largely broken. The area was affected by the national growth in unemployment and the depression, culminating in the General Strike of 1926. Unemployment mounted as manufacturing industries lost their competitiveness and the boom years of the war came to an end.

Despite the prevailing economic gloom, life in Dudley continued with such events as Sunday School processions, mayoral parades at the beginning of each civic year in November, Armistice celebrations, and the first Dudley Carnival in 1929. These, of course, were the years before the National Health Service, and fund-raising events, especially to help the Guest Hospital, were quite common, such as the bazaar attended by the Duke and Duchess of York in 1925, and a cricket club carnival and fête in 1926.

Several national events were marked in Dudley during this time. George V's silver jubilee in 1935 was a cause for national celebration, but only a year later he was dead, and the country greeted a new monarch, Edward VIII, who was proclaimed king in January 1936. The nation was soon shaken by the abdication crisis, and George VI was proclaimed king in December 1936, and crowned in May the following year.

These decades also saw visits to Dudley from members of the royal family, marked with various celebrations. Edward, Prince of Wales came to Dudley in 1923 and again in 1927, and his brother and sister-in-law, the Duke and Duchess of York, later King and Queen, visited in 1925. The visit of the Prince of Wales to Dudley and the Black Country in 1923 was probably part of his investigations into unemployment and the problems faced by ex-servicemen. In 1927 he was again in the area, this time to open the new road from Birmingham to Wolverhampton. The Duke and Duchess of York's visit included the Guest Hospital and the Guest Hospital Bazaar and Old English Fayre at the National Projectile Factory. There was also a visit by Princess Mary in 1930, to open the Guest Hospital extensions.

The First World War also continued to cast its shadow over the 1920s and '30s. War memorials, such as the one at Woodside, were unveiled, and the new town hall, with its war memorial tower, was opened by the prime minister, Stanley Baldwin, in 1928. This building was made possible by a bequest of Mr Brooke Robinson, and later included the Brooke Robinson Museum too. Other noteworthy events of the period included the victory of Dorothy Round in the Ladies' Singles Championship at Wimbledon in 1934, which was a cause for much celebration in her home town of Dudley, and opening of the new Odeon cinema and Dudley Zoo in 1937.

On a civic level, improvements were being considered for education, municipal housing, streets and health. Health provision began to be improved following the gift of The Firs, Dixons Green, to the town by Sir George Bean in about 1922 and the opening of a child welfare clinic there. There was some municipal housing provided, for example on the Brewery Fields site, and the experimental iron houses in Ernest Road, built between 1925 and 1927. There were problems with a lack of suitable land for development because Dudley was effectively land-locked, an island of Worcestershire surrounded by Staffordshire. Moves to remedy this began with the purchase of the Priory Estate from the Earl of Dudley in 1924. There were plans for its development from 1927 and the corporation were able to proceed with these after the extension of the borough boundaries following the Dudley Corporation Act of 1928. The first foundation stones for houses on the Priory Estate were laid in 1929 and development followed apace: the problems of sub-standard housing could then be tackled. The first slum clearance scheme began in the Birmingham Street area in 1930, and was followed by other areas during the period leading up to the Second World War. There were improvements in health provision, such as refuse collection; in education with the provision of new schools and the opening of the new technical college in 1936. The Birmingham New Road was opened in 1927, King Street was widened, Castle Hill and Trindle Road were improved and a bypass, the Broadway, was opened in 1935. There was also the opening of the new Priory Park and the sports centre in Tipton Road in 1932, to encourage participation in recreational activities and sports. The new Council House was opened by the Duke of Kent in 1935.

These two decades, and especially the second, from 1929, can be described as a period of change and development in Dudley, and, with hindsight, as a brief respite between two catastrophic world wars.

Dudley St John Ambulance Corps, drawn up for a parade on the former vegetable market, on the corner of Stone Street and Priory Street, c. 1920. This photograph is not dated, but it is certainly before the commencement of the building of the town hall, the foundation stone of which was laid on 17 April 1926. The corps are probably preparing for the mayoral church parade: they received invitations to take part in 1920, 1921 and 1922. These were held in mid-November at the beginning of the civic year, following the election of the mayor. The mayor, members of the corporation, officials, the police, the fire brigade, and other organisations took part. On each occasion the parade formed up in Stone Street and the vegetable market.

Group of employees outside Goodwin, Foster Brown Ltd, Parsons Street, *c.* 1920. It is believed that they were preparing to take part in a Wolverhampton carnival, hence the firm's vans are decorated and the ladies have collecting tins. The man on the far left is probably Fred Hackett. Some of the other people present are Ted Yardley (immediately on the left of the ladies), and on the right of the group, Gertrude Baker, Joe Harris and William Clayton. The company, a wholesale grocer and flour merchants, was incorporated in 1897, the original partners being Mr T.H. Goodwin, flour merchant, George Foster, retail shop proprietor, and George Brown, yeast merchant. They made Goodwin's extra self raising flour, with the baby picture on each bag.

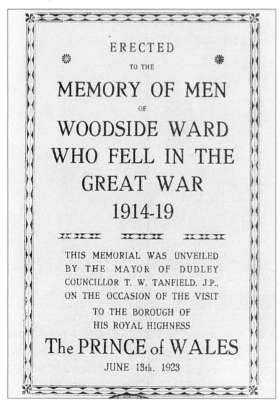

ERECTED
TO THE
MEMORY OF MEN
OF
WOODSIDE WARD
WHO FELL IN THE
GREAT WAR
1914-19

THIS MEMORIAL WAS UNVEILED
BY THE MAYOR OF DUDLEY
COUNCILLOR T. W. TANFIELD, J.P.,
ON THE OCCASION OF THE VISIT
TO THE BOROUGH OF
HIS ROYAL HIGHNESS
The PRINCE of WALES
JUNE 13th, 1923

Front page of a programme for the unveiling of Woodside's Great War memorial, 13 June 1923. The mayor, Councillor T.W. Tanfield, unveiled the memorial on the same day as the Prince of Wales's visit to Dudley, although the Prince did not attend this event. The programme includes the names of Woodside men who died and the order of the ceremony. The memorial consists of an obelisk mounted on a platform of three broad steps of Cornish granite with bronze panels on the sides, one with an inscription and three with the names of the fallen. Erected by public subscription, it originally stood on the main road at Holly Hall, and is now in St Augustine's churchyard.

Dudley Market Place (right) decorated for the visit of the Prince of Wales, and the Prince of Wales arriving outside the Town Hall (below), Wednesday 13 June 1923. On his visit, he demonstrated his concerns for employment, industry and ex-servicemen. His first stop in the borough was at the Netherton Ironworks of N. Hingley & Sons Ltd. He went on to open the new drill hall of the 268th Battery Royal Field Artillery (Territorial Army) in Trinity Road and to inspect a guard of honour at the town hall, provided by the 7th Battalion Worcestershire Regiment. The Prince then proceeded to the works of A. Harper, Sons & Bean, motor car manufacturers, at Waddams Pool. There, he inspected the large number of ex-servicemen employed by the firm and met the directors. Afterwards he met members of the local British Legion and ex-servicemen, as well as widows and children of those killed in the First World War. Next he visited the Guest Hospital, meeting the trustees, hospital committee, staff and patients, before leaving for Wolver-hampton. In honour of the visit there was a cricket match at the county ground, Dudley v. Old Hill, and music in the parks in the afternoon and evening, followed by a dance at the Palais de Danse, Wolverhampton Street, and aerial fireworks provided by the Earl of Dudley from the castle keep.

St Augustine's, Holly Hall, Sunday School festival outdoor procession, 13 July 1924, with the choir and part of the procession in Stourbridge Road. The festival included outdoor processions at 10 a.m. and 2 p.m. choral eucharist at 11, a service in Holly Hall park, or in the church if wet, in the afternoon, and at 6.30 p.m. festival evensong. There were thirty-five communicants at the 11 a.m. service and collections for the day totalled £33 6s 7½d. The Old Coach and Horses, Stourbridge Road, whose licensee was John Arthur Swann, can be seen in the picture, and also the tramlines of the Dudley to Stourbridge tram service, which was replaced by buses in 1930.

The Duke and Duchess of York with young patients outside the Guest Hospital, during their visit to the Black Country, 4 June 1925. They had earlier visited Messrs Lench's works in Blackheath, and Stevens & Williams Ltd in Brierley Hill, before going on to Himley Hall. On their return to Dudley the Duke and Duchess visited the Guest Hospital, and the Guest Hospital Bazaar and Old English Fayre, held at the National Projectile Factory. This event was part of an appeal to raise £10,000 to clear the hospital's outstanding debts. The Duchess received cheques on behalf of the hospital, and the Duke drove the engine on the Broome Miniature Railway. The fayre and other appeals realised more than £14,000 for the hospital's funds.

A draft of a poster advertising Dudley Cricket Carnival and Fête on 2 August 1926 at the County Cricket Ground, in aid of the Guest Hospital. Between 6,000 and 7,000 visitors flocked there to see a variety of events, ranging from a schoolboys' high jump competition, with prizes presented by Joe Darby, champion jumper, to the ladies' ankle competion, won by Miss Pearson! There was also free vaudeville entertainment and a tug-of-war competition for local teams, which was won by the Shakespeare Hotel, Stafford Street. The biggest fundraiser was the competition to win a cricket bat used by the Worcestershire cricketer Jack Hobbs, and presented by Fred Root, the Dudley cricketer. Of the £250 raised, £100 came from this competition alone.

665

DUDLEY EDUCATION COMMITTEE

SCHOOL OF ARTS AND CRAFTS

ST. JAMES' ROAD, DUDLEY

Principal - IVO SHAW

The NEXT SESSION COMMENCES MONDAY, 13th SEPTEMBER, 1926

DAY & EVENING CLASSES FOR DRAWING & PAINTING LIFE

(PORTRAITURE & COSTUME)

Designing & Craft Work, specially adapted to the requirements of Local Industries.

TRADE CLASSES

These are Conducted by Practical Teachers,

AND INCLUDE CLASSES FOR:

Decorative Metal Work,
Ornamental Wrought Iron,
Plumbing and Lead Work,
Typography,
Black and White Design,

Carpentry and Joinery,
Cabinetmaking, Housepainting,
Decorating, Signwriting,
Silversmithing, Enamelling,
Dress Designing, Embroidery,

Leatherwork, &c.

FEES: Day Classes from **15/-** Evening from **3/6**

SCHOLARSHIPS are awarded to Students attending Trade Classes.

Prospectus & Leaflets, giving further information as to Courses of Study, Fees, Scholarships, etc., may be obtained from the Principal of the School, or from

J. WHALEY, Director of Education.

Education Offices, Dudley.

Blocksidge, Printer, Dudley. 18351

A poster advertising classes at the School of Arts and Crafts, St James's Road, September 1926. The school was established in 1884. Ivo Shaw was principal from 1913 to 1947, and was responsible for organising the school and teaching. He was keen to link the work of the school with the needs of local industry. Day and evening classes were held in general art work and evening classes in branches of metalwork and woodwork. Most of the craft teachers were practised men with responsible positions in relevant industries. Two famous graduates of the school, taught by Mr Shaw, were the local artist Percy Shakespeare and James Whale, who later went to Hollywood (see page 43).

Work in progress on the reconstruction of Cinder Bank, Netherton, probably 1926. The properties on the right still exist. The junction with Swan Street can be seen with the Hope Tavern on the corner and the premises of Harry Harper, picture framer, and possibly those of Henry Newbury, tailor. The corporation entered into an agreement with Tarmac Ltd of Ettingshall for the resurfacing of Cinder Bank Road between Pear Tree Lane and Grazebrooks Crossing in the early part of 1926. The work was to cost £920 14s 4d.

Part of the procession of St John's Sunday School festival, 12 July 1928, in Dixons Green at the junction with St John's Road. There were two processions of the Sunday School scholars around the parish that day as well as church services. Offerings of flowers, eggs, and fruit which were brought to the flower service in the afternoon were sent to the Guest Hospital and the infirmary. The house on the corner is probably The Hawthorns, the residence of Hugh Smith JP, a surgeon. The Firs is behind the wall, beyond the trees. This was donated to the town by Sir George Bean in about 1922, to be used as a maternity and child welfare clinic.

The opening of the town hall buildings by the prime minister, Stanley Baldwin, 16 October 1928. Left, Mr Baldwin addressing the gathering from the platform, and below, Mr and Mrs Baldwin at the entrance to the war memorial tower. This complex included the coroner's court, sessions court and Brooke Robinson Museum, as well as the town hall and memorial tower, inscribed with the names of all 700 Dudley men who died in the First World War. The opening ceremony was attended by the Earl and Countess of Dudley, Lord and Lady Ednam, Wyndham Baldwin, son of the prime minister, Lady Rosslyn, mayors and mayoresses of neighbouring authorities, chairmen of local urban councils, town clerks and clerks of other authorities. The prime minister was invited by Alderman Adshead, chairman of the Patriotic Committee, to open the wrought-iron and gilded gates to the memorial chamber and to light the eternal lamp of remembrance, which was to be kept burning as a symbol of the sacrifice of the fallen. Mr Baldwin was then handed a presentation key by W. Alexander Harvey, representing Harveys & Wicks of Birmingham, architects. On the right of the picture below are the mayor, Councillor F.J. Ballard, the mayoress, Mrs Ballard, and the recorder of Dudley, Mr Herbert Davy. On the left are an unidentified person, possibly Alderman Adshead, and W. Alexander Harvey.

A group of pupils at work in the botany laboratory at Dudley Girls' High School, Priory Road, taken for the school prospectus, *c.* 1928. According to this, the school had a large assembly hall, fitted up as a gymnasium, a dining room, a library, two well-equipped laboratories, a studio and numerous well-ventilated classrooms. Outside were a hockey field, three grass and two asphalt tennis courts and a playground. The curriculum included scripture, English language and literature, history, geography, French, Latin, mathematics, chemistry, physics, botany, zoology, hygiene, nature study, drawing, needlework, handiwork, cookery, class singing, eurhythmics, gymnastics and dancing, as well as German, Italian and Greek, if desired. The school was fee paying at this time, but scholarships were available.

Dudley's first carnival, September 1929. Seated are the mayor, Alderman F.J. Ballard, the carnival queen, Miss Joyce E. Raybould, and the mayoress, Mrs Ballard, and standing behind them the carnival queen's attendants, Miss Maisy Lane, Miss Irene Clarke, Miss Ruby Harley, and on the far right Miss Doris Simms and members of the carnival committee. The official opening of the carnival and the crowning of the carnival queen by the mayor took place on the Monday at the castle. Various events took place over the week, including football and cricket matches, carnival dances, ox roasts and a swimming gala. It was very well supported, raising over £5,000 for charity. The climax of the week was the Grand Carnival and Trades procession on Saturday 21 September.

The Wayfarers cricket team, *c.* 1930. The Wayfarers – 'A Band of Strolling Cricketers' – were a touring cricket side. From *The Way of the Wayfarer*, the chronicle of the team's activities, it seems that the team's tours took them mainly to the Isle of Wight and Hampshire, and that it was accompanied on these trips by its friends. The first tour was in August 1913, to the Isle of Wight. Seated on the extreme left of the front row of this photograph is Fred Root, the famous Dudley cricketer, who played for Worcestershire from 1923 to 1931. Horace Wainwright is on the extreme left of the back row; third row from the front, extreme left is Arthur Betteridge, third from left, Tom Williams; second row: second from left is Mr Wilkinson, and fourth from right is Mr J.E. Cartwright; and fourth from the right in the front row is Joe Lewis.

Advertisement for Old Sol, from the *Dudley Official Handbook*, *c.* 1932. Old Sol was a furniture, floor and lino polish manufactured by Raybould, Whitehouse & Co. Ltd, manufacturing chemists, of the Reform Works, Wellington Road. The firm was founded in 1878 by Joseph Raybould and was based in New Street until 1885. The founder's son, George Raybould, later ran the company in partnership with his brother-in-law, Joseph Whitehouse. By the time Mr Raybould took over the whole of the business, on the death of Joseph Whitehouse in 1934, Old Sol, with a drawing of the sun, was the firm's trademark. This advertisement had been used since at least 1929 and was probably inspired by the total eclipse of the sun in 1927.

Hall Street by night, looking towards the Market Place, 1934. This is one of a series of photographs by the Revo Electric Co. Ltd of Tividale, Tipton, and shows the recently installed electric street lighting. This installation was part of a scheme by the corporation to improve street lighting, including the replacement of gas by electric, which began in 1933. The work in Hall Street had been completed by the end of 1934. Revo Electric, formerly Cable Accessories Co. Ltd, was established in 1907, with twelve workmen, to manufacture underground electrical equipment. By 1927 it had a new name, works covering 40 acres and 2,000 employees. It became a public company in 1936 and by the 1960s was part of the DuPont group.

Headquarters of the Netherton men's branch of Toc H, Bagley's Lane, Netherton, June 1934. Toc H began as a soldiers' club in Talbot House, from which its name derives, in Poperinghe, Belgium, in 1915. The movement was revived in 1919 by its founder, the Rev. Philip (Tubby) Clayton. Its aim was to continue the common service of wartime by helping those less fortunate in the community. The Netherton men's branch was formed in 1933, and the first meetings were at Church House, Netherton. This cottage was used for meetings from 30 June 1933 until January 1944, when the organisation moved to their new meeting place at 53 Griffin Street. They continued to meet there until they disbanded in May 1998.

Miss Dorothy Round (on the right) and her opponent, Miss Helen Jacobs of the USA, going out to play in the Ladies' Singles Final at Wimbledon, 7 July 1934. Miss Round won 6–2, 5–7, 6–3. She also won the Mixed Doubles Championship with her partner R. Miki of Japan. Dorothy was the daughter of Mr J.B. Round of Park Road, Dudley, and an old girl of Dudley Girls' High School. On her return to Dudley after her Wimbledon victory there was a public welcome, and a children's cot was provided at the Guest Hospital in her name. Dorothy Round won the Singles Championship for the second time in 1937. She married Dr Douglas Leigh Little in 1938 and died in 1982.

Street cleansing vehicles, *c.* 1935. The central figures are Sidney Skitt, chief sanitary inspector and cleansing superintendent, and Mr W. Fellows, assistant cleansing superintendent. The function of street cleansing was transferred from the Streets Committee to the Health Committee from 1 July 1934, and improved. Collection by horse-drawn open carts was discontinued and street refuse was swept and loaded into dustbins fitted to an orderly truck, as here. The refuse was then emptied into the vehicles used for house refuse collection and taken to a controlled tip. These Freighter Refuse Collection vehicles, manufactured by Messrs Shelvoke and Drewery Ltd of Letchworth, replaced refuse collection by horse-drawn vehicles and cost £692 each.

Official opening of The Broadway by the mayor, 1 May 1935. The deputy mayor, Alderman J.H. Molyneux, the town clerk, Mr G.C.V. Cant and the borough engineer, Mr F.H. Gibbons, are also pictured here. This brief ceremony took place at the point where The Broadway converges with the Sedgley Road, in the presence of other members of Dudley Corporation and others interested in the project of a bypass road from Castle Hill to Burton Road. This was first considered as early as 1924 as part of the development of the Priory Estate. The first portion, from Ednam Road to Priory Road was built in 1931, and the second phase, to Burton Road, in 1932. The road was named The Broadway, in November 1933.

Civic parade in Wolverhampton Street returning from a service of thanksgiving for the silver jubilee of King George V and Queen Mary, 6 May 1935. The parade made its way to land near Paganel Drive, where the 268th Dudley Battery territorials fired a royal salute and A Company of 7th Battalion Worcestershire Regiment fired a 'feu de joie'. The Earl of Dudley opened the castle grounds and provided a programme of entertainment. There were bonfires, a beacon at Shavers End, which was one of a chain, a torchlight procession and a ball at the town hall. There was extra relief for the unemployed, gifts for the elderly and blind, and a tea for schoolchildren who were all presented with jubilee souvenirs.

Dudley Grammar School boys on their way to the first school commemoration service at St Thomas's church, 20 July 1936. The service, which commemorated the opening of the school, was conducted by the vicar, who was also vice-chairman of the school governors, and was attended by the headmaster, Mr D.C. Temple, Mrs Temple, the masters and boys, as well as several governors, the director of education, parents and friends and a party of sixteen girls from Dudley Girls' High School. This service was part of 'Commemoration Fortnight' covering the period between the end of examinations and the last day of term. The school's final commemoration service was held on 23 July 1975 prior to the school's amalgamation with Dudley Girls' High School.

Dudley territorials, *c.* 1937. Ted Woolams is in the centre of the back row, and Tommy Turley is on the extreme right of the front row. By this period the Territorial Army in Dudley consisted of the 268th Field Battery Royal Artillery TA whose headquarters were at the Riding School in Trinity Road, and A Company 7th Battalion Worcestershire Regiment TA, whose headquarters were in Trindle Road. The officer commanding 268th Field Battery was Maj J.G. Stewart Smith, with officers, Capt F.H. Green, 2nd Lt F.W. Harris and 2nd Lt R.S. Roberts. The officers of A Company were Capt F.J. Somers, and Lt E.F. Tomkinson. There were a canteen and recreation room with billiards at both headquarters.

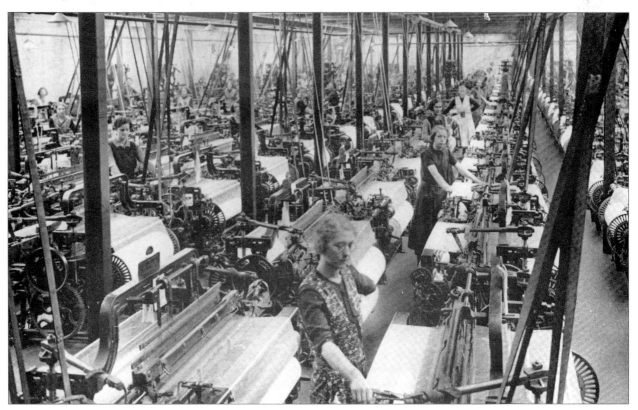

No. 1 weaving shed, Scrim Manufacturing Co. Ltd, 1937. This photograph is taken from the firm's brochure, published in 1937 to coincide with George VI's coronation and to give a pictorial record of their manufacturing progress. Scrim Manufacturing, based in London Fields, were weavers, bleachers and finishers of cotton. The brochure contains an aerial photograph of the works and of machinery used, as well as pictures of some of their finished products. The firm claimed that the machinery showcased in this brochure was the result of the most 'up to date scientific textile engineering'. Scrim Manufacturing was in existence at least as early as 1924, when they were at Tetnall Street, and moved to London Fields some time between 1925 and 1928.

The Odeon cinema, Castle Hill, 12 July 1937. This was the last cinema to be built in Dudley and is shown here almost completed. The poster on the side of the building is advertising the opening night, which was to take place shortly, and the board in front gives details of the architect, contractor, sub-contractors and suppliers. The architect was Henry W. Weedon of Birmingham, who was by this time the consultant architect to Odeon Theatres Ltd, and was largely responsible for their distinctive house style. The general contractors were Housing Ltd, public works contractors of Black Heath, and the decoration was by Decorative Crafts Ltd, Birmingham. The cinema cost £60,000 to build and could seat 2,000 people.

Guests at the gala opening of the Odeon cinema, 28 July 1937. Standing, left to right: H.W. Weedon, architect; H. Parkes, Director (Odeon Cinemas); H. Uglow, Housing Ltd; J.L. Hillman, Mayor of Dudley; Oscar Deutsch, governing director and founder of Odeon Cinemas; W.G. Alcock, Director; the page who presented the ladies' bouquets; and C.A. Crathorn, the resident manager. Their wives and the mayoress, Mrs J.L. Hillman, are seated in front. The opening ceremony was performed by the mayor and a full programme of a film and British Movietone News followed. The programme for the Thursday, Friday and Saturday of the opening week was *Beloved Enemy*, starring Merle Oberon, and *Sporting Love*, with Stanley Lupino.

Shetland ponies and a camel arriving at Dudley Zoo, Thursday 15 April 1937. These were among the first consignment of animals transferred to Dudley from Oxford Zoo. The very first inhabitants were three peacocks given by the Duke of Sutherland, which had arrived earlier that same week. The animals from Oxford Zoo formed the nucleus of the Dudley Zoo collection, but they were soon followed by two young elephants from Mysore in India, with bona fide mahouts, called Maharanee and Yuvarajah. They completed their journey by rail, being met by the Earl of Dudley, his sons and others. Four lions and wolves arrived later, also to be met by the Earl, followed by two polar bears and five tigers, including two cubs. Bison were to come from Canada and other animals, such as sea lions, zebras, monkeys, bears, penguins, flamingoes, and pelicans, originated from Hamburg

Zoo, where all the stock was for sale. By the time the zoo opened there were fifty to sixty kinds of mammals and over a hundred types of birds. In total there were around a thousand animals. Pictured below is the zoo's manager, who had been associated with Oxford Zoo since 1933, when it had been taken over by Mr Cooper, and was its last manager. This photograph also shows the zoo entrance still under construction. The zoo opened on 6 May 1937, although it was still unfinished.

Babies born on Coronation Day, 1937. On 23 July 1937, at the Junior Conservative Club, Priory Road, Mr Dudley Joel MP presented each of the babies born on George VI's coronation day with a £5 note and a silver spoon. The event took place during the interval in an entertainment presented by a party of 'Primrose Buds', twenty-six children of the Junior Primrose League. The six mothers and babies took pride of place on the platform and included Mrs Taylor and her daughter Elizabeth, Mrs Parkes and Sheila Rosemary, Mrs Bird and her son George Dudley, Mrs Townsend and Margaret Rose, and Mrs Parkes. Mrs Taylor had the double distinction of having had a child on Jubilee Day 1935 as well!

Turning the Earl of Dudley's statue, 7 May 1939. The statue of the 1st Earl of Dudley (1817–85) was unveiled on 25 April 1888. It weighs about 6 tons and was sculpted from Sicilian marble. It was turned to face the Market Place instead of looking towards the Conservative Club in Castle Hill, to comply with the wishes of the Earl of Dudley and the Ward family. A mobile crane, manoeuvred into position by a traction engine, lifted and replaced the statue, after the base had been moved on a slipway. The statue was moved a distance of 6 yds to the centre of a large traffic island at the top of the hill, as part of the Castle Hill Improvement Scheme.

4. War and Peace

Business girls walking along Priory Road on their way to work during the first week of war, September 1939, carrying their gas masks. Once war was announced pedestrians were required to carry their respirators at all times; they did this a little self-consciously at first, but later with increasing apathy. They could be carried under the individual's arm or, as seen here, over their shoulder on a strap. More than 63,000 respirators had been distributed to the populace since 1938. Siren warnings would signal the alarm if enemy aircraft appeared overhead.

Introduction

The Second World War dominated the 1940s. From 1940 to 1945 everyday life in Britain was secondary to the war effort, but despite the hardships of rationing and fear of the enemy, morale remained high and determination to defeat Hitler did not falter. From 1946 to 1949 society was affected by the changes brought about by reaction to the austerity of the previous five years, and the desire of ordinary people to build a better life. Respect for women, who had undertaken hard manual labour whilst their menfolk had been fighting, had grown and working-class men had lost their awe of the upper class as they fought alongside them.

The scene was set for conflict following Hitler's invasion of Czechoslovakia, and in 1938 preparations were being made for war. Dudley complied with Home Office instructions and trenches were dug to shelter 10 per cent of the population in the event of air raids. The government also arranged for the distribution of gas masks, should a state of emergency be declared. War had been anticipated throughout 1939, and in Dudley recruitment for civil defence as well as the armed forces had taken place. By the time war was declared, Dudley felt it was as prepared as it could be, ARP personnel had been appointed, civic buildings were sandbagged, the blackout was organised. At the outbreak of war Dudley Council announced that all house building, redevelopment and road schemes were halted. The only exceptions were the new fire station and police buildings which were already under construction, and eventually opened on 2 October 1941.

In 1940 Hitler tried, unsuccessfully, to destroy the air force: the ensuing Battle of Britain was a famous victory and, in gratitude, many towns including Dudley raised enormous amounts of money to purchase Spitfires. From 1940 onwards air raids became more frequent, but because of a ban on reporting the details it was not until 1944 that Dudley learned the extent of the damage: 358 alerts had been recorded in Dudley between the first raid in June 1940 and the beginning of 1944, but only a small number of bombs were dropped. A few houses were badly damaged and demolished but most were repairable. One bomb landed near St Thomas's church, demolishing a nearby public house. There were a few casualties but only one fatality, a Mrs George Marlow. As a result of the air raids Dudley improved its civil defence facilities, by providing more shelters during 1942.

Food rationing was introduced in 1940, and entreaties were made for local people to 'Dig for Victory' and grow food. By 1941 two British restaurants had opened in Dudley, essentially community feeding centres enabling the populace to save their rations. Various salvage campaigns were introduced from 1941 – kitchen waste to feed pigs and poultry, scrap iron for war weapons, for which railings were taken down from local churchyards, and in 1942 a waste paper salvage operation during which Dudley collected 126 tons.

By the end of 1941 women were conscripted, either to join the services, to undertake war work or work in factories. Wartime nurseries were created to help women with childcare during this time and in 1943 school meals were introduced for children. There was a shortage of miners during the war, so 10 per cent of young men conscripted after 1943 were directed to work in the coal mines as 'Bevin boys'.

Shortages began to bite in 1942. Strict fuel controls were in place, there was no petrol for private motoring, people were asked to take fewer baths and to restrict water levels, and clothes were rationed. New clothes were plain and people became experts at making new garments from old cloth. By 1943 only utility furniture was being made and priority was given to those who had been bombed. Newspapers were restricted to four pages.

Following the D-Day invasion of Europe in 1944 civil defence duties were reduced, the Home Guard stood down, the blackout relaxed and people once again enjoyed street lights. War ended in Europe on 8 May 1945 and Japan surrendered on 14 August. Massive celebrations took place in the streets throughout the country. The war over, Churchill dissolved parliament and the Labour party won a landslide victory, on a platform of increased nationalisation and the creation of a welfare state, which promised government help to those in need. 1944 had already seen the introduction of Butler's Education Act, promising secondary education for all children. In 1947 the school leaving age was raised to fifteen.

After the war there was an acute housing shortage. Returning soldiers, evacuees and those whose houses had been destroyed in bombing raids all wanted homes, so many authorities, including Dudley, built prefabs as a short-term measure as building materials were in short supply. Assisted by government grants, local councils built over 80 per cent of houses erected in the postwar '40s. Food shortages continued, because of a world food crisis, and bread and potato rationing were introduced. Harvest camps continued even up to 1949, farmers needing the help of schoolchildren because of a shortage of agricultural labour. Utility furniture and household appliances were rationed until 1950 and sweets continued to be rationed until February 1953.

The National Health Service came into being in 1948, to provide comprehensive health care free at the point of delivery. It dramatically reduced infant mortality, as until then two-thirds of mothers were not attended by a doctor. An immunisation programme was introduced to reduce the spread of disease.

Meanwhile social and technological changes taking place world-wide would have far reaching implications for Britain. Tower blocks of flats were being built in France by Le Corbusier, the first electronic digital computer was installed in the USA, and transistors were invented to replace valves, which would ultimately lead to miniature radios and smaller computers. Television broadcasts had resumed after the war, but only 14,000 licences had been issued by 1945; television was not to reach the Midlands until 1949.

Fitting children with respirators, September 1938. Children's respirators were supplied direct to schools and the head teachers were responsible for their safekeeping. Adult respirators were distributed and fitted, by volunteers, at local polling stations from Wednesday 29 September and also at the ARP centre in Stafford Street where the volunteers were helped by sixty girls, sent by the employment exchange. By the following day more than 1,000 volunteers were involved. The distribution of gas masks was suspended during the first week in October 1938, not because war had been averted but because the authorities ran out; it was expected that everyone should receive one within the next two weeks as the prime minister warned that ARP measures must be continued despite the declaration of peace. In May 1939 householders were asked to produce their gas masks for inspection as reports of their being abused (used as footballs in the street) had been given. The subsequent inspection found that such reports had been greatly exaggerated. A new census of schoolchildren was ordered to ensure that numbers and correct sizes were available. During the first week of war 2,000 baby helmets were issued, and by mid-September the full quota of baby respirators had been received and classes held for parents giving instruction in their fitting and use.

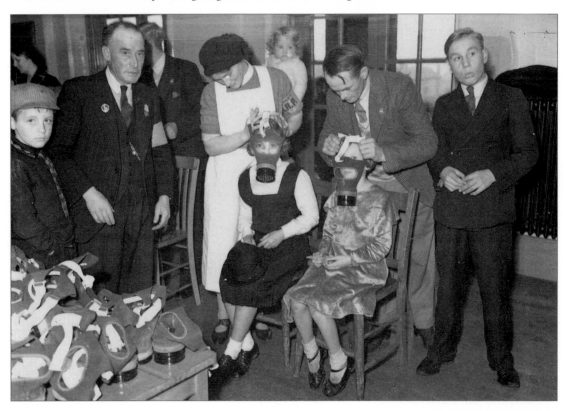

Assembling respirators at the ARP centre, September 1938. Gas masks were distributed in 1938 during the crisis in Europe when war seemed imminent. Dudley's consignment of 57,000 gas masks arrived in two 5 ton railway containers and two Home Office vans during the last week in September. A further delivery was expected, as following a census it was anticipated that 65,000 masks in total would be needed. The masks, available in small, medium or large sizes, were packed in airtight tin boxes in batches of fifty, and the filtering canisters were packed separately. It was estimated that in an emergency they could be assembled at a rate of two per second.

A policeman on point duty during the first week of war, September 1939. As soon as war was declared on 3 September 1939 emergency procedures were put in place. Here the policeman outside Burtons on Hall Street has replaced his helmet with a steel hat, and is carrying a respirator. Blackout procedures were also adopted, and ARP volunteers visited householders informing them of the restrictions.

ARP digging trenches, September 1938. The photograph on the left was taken at Sweet Turf, Netherton. Preparations for war were being made during the European crisis of September and October. Following a Home Office order to provide trenches so that 10 per cent of the population might be able to take cover within three days, the ARP began digging trenches on open land in and around the towns of Dudley and Netherton on Monday 27 September. Mass public meetings were held to explain to the townspeople why these measure were being taken, and the corporation made an urgent appeal for volunteers. By October only 1,950 recruits had volunteered, and a further 4,000 were needed. The first trenches were dug on cleared land at Woodside, Netherton, and at Birmingham Street and Fisher Street in Dudley. About 200 men were used, including all Dudley Corporation workmen and eighty unemployed men. The cost of digging these trenches was £593. The standard measurements for trenches were 5 ft 6 in deep by 4 ft 6 in wide at the surface and 2 ft 6 in wide at the floor. The total depth, including the parapet, was 7 ft. The sides were to be reinforced with wire netting and wooden posts. Trenches had to be preserved and maintained in good order by government order. The ARP were also given other tasks, such as painting kerb corners and curbs around traffic islands white to help traffic in the event of a blackout.

Above: 'Dudley girl ambulance drivers', 14 October 1939. Women were beginning to take over jobs that would formerly have been done by men. Dudley was short of 200 ARP ambulance drivers in May, but by October all of those posts had been filled by women. Traders' vans were used as makeshift ARP ambulances, and as well as driving these heavy vehicles the ladies were quite capable, as seen here, of donning protective overalls to carry out maintenance work on the engine. One ambulance was equipped as an operating theatre, carrying dressings and surgical instruments, two nurses and one doctor. The other ambulances were fitted with brackets to hold four to six stretchers. There were ten vehicles available for full-time use, and ten more on call.

Shop closing hours, 11 November 1939. Dudley's shopkeepers announced their decision to continue with early closing, at 6 p.m. on Monday, Tuesday and Thursday and 7 p.m. on Friday and Saturday, out of consideration to staff and the public alike, as a safety measure during the blackout. The traders felt that the public response to early closing had been favourable and appealed to everyone to shop as early as possible. Although the council had given permission for longer hours it was felt that there would not be enough demand for staying open later.

IMPORTANT NOTICE
ABOUT DUDLEY
SHOP CLOSING HOURS

The Principal Dudley Shops have decided to continue the Early Closing Hours of 6 p.m. on Monday, Tuesday and Thursday and 7 p.m. on Friday and Saturday.

They appreciate the splendid manner in which the Shopping Public have responded to these new hours during the last few weeks, and by continuing these times, the Traders believe they are interpreting the wishes of the vast majority of their customers, having due regard for the safety and comfort both of their staffs and the public. They appeal therefore for everyone to shop as early as possible.

Representative of the firms who are closing at the above hours are F. W. Cook Ltd., Edward Grey Ltd., Marks & Spencer Ltd., Geo. Mason Ltd., Samuel Hill Ltd., and many other important establishments.

The Dudley Co-operative Society Shops are keeping to the above hours except on Mondays, when they will close at 5 p.m.

This advertisement is issued on behalf of the other Traders by F. W. Cook Ltd., High Street, Dudley.

GAS

Dudley has
rely on Gas
economy and

It is the wis
that this su
in war-time
anxious for
value for the

If you have
let us know-
experience ar

AT YO

If you require the m
to make the m
special Home S
supervision of
matters. Mak
Telephone Dudl

 ADVERTISEMENT
AND DISTRICT (

THE

THE FOUNTA

THIS YEAR-
A GREETING OF

ORDER YOU
Do not forget the S

CHRIS
and P
(Order

**CALEND
FOUNTAI
WRI**

SHOWROOM
(IN BASEME

SHOP EAR
AND SECURE

 3/5, FOUNTA

NATIONAL SERVICE

RECRUITING WEEK

MAY 15th to 20th, 1939.

NATIONAL SERVICE PARADE

Saturday, 20th May, 1939

2.30 p.m. to 6 p.m.

GRAND PROCESSION

Starting from NETHERTON and WOODSIDE via MARKET PLACE to SPORTS CENTRE, BIRMINGHAM ROAD.

A.R.P., MILITARY AND FITNESS DISPLAYS

WILL BE GIVEN AT THE SPORTS CENTRE.

THE CIVIL DEFENCE OF DUDLEY, your Home and your Family is Your Responsibility.

HAVE YOU ENROLLED?

If not, enrol at:—

65, HIGH STREET, DUDLEY (open May 15th to 20th).

A.R.P. HEADQUARTERS, STAFFORD STREET,

— Or —

MINISTRY OF LABOUR EMPLOYMENT EXCHANGE, PARSONS STREET.

2,000 VOLUNTEERS WANTED

NEXT WEEK

Will YOU be one of them?

National Service Recruiting Week, 15–20 May 1939. The authorities believed that as Dudley would be manufacturing munitions it would be the target of extensive enemy bombing if hostilities broke out. As a result an intensive recruiting campaign for civil defence volunteers was instituted. Recruiting headquarters were opened in the former Grainger & Smith premises at 65 High Street for the duration of the campaign, and there was extensive publicity both in the local press and by posters. Volunteers were required for the following personnel: VAD workers, air raid wardens, first aid workers, ambulance service drivers and attendants, rescue and demolition workers and decontamination squad members. All the posts for car drivers and messengers had been filled, but there was a considerable shortfall for other workers.

Territorial Army, Market Place, 20 May 1939. The culmination of National Service recruiting week was a massed parade of regular and territorial army units and ARP services, followed by a demonstration at the Sports Centre. High Street was closed to traffic for one and a half hours while the parade of about 1,500 personnel passed through the town centre. Crowds lined the route to watch the spectacle. Over 5,000 watched the demonstration at the sports ground, which included the 265th Field Battery of the 67th Field Regiment Royal Artillery (TA) firing cartridges from four 4.5 in howitzer guns. Its captain hoped to recruit 318 more men to bring the battery up to full strength; 100 men had enlisted since Easter but its present strength was only 230.

The arrival of German refugee Kurt Flossman at Dudley Grammar School, 30 January 1939. This image shows fourteen-year-old Kurt, a Protestant refugee from Berlin, with his new school friends. His father had been a commercial traveller who had died in 1937. Kurt had made his way across Europe to England and had been staying at a refugee camp in Dovercourt before his sponsorship by the grammar school students. The students would have to find £50 per year for four years (until Kurt was eighteen) for his fees and expenses, but his clothes were sponsored by local firms. Kurt already spoke English and settled in well at the grammar school, quickly making new friends and becoming a member of the scouts.

FOLLOW YOUR TRADE IN THE FIGHTING FORCES

Young men with experience in various branches of engineering, building, motor transport, electrical engineering, and certain other occupations, are required for immediate service IN THEIR TRADES in the Royal Navy, the Army and the Royal Air Force. Men of or above the age specified for their occupation in the Schedule of Reserved Occupations will not be accepted.

MEN EMPLOYED UPON URGENT GOVERNMENT CONTRACTS ARE STRONGLY ADVISED TO REMAIN AT THEIR PRESENT WORK

Go to a Recruiting Office or get information at an Employment Exchange

A recruiting poster, 30 September 1939. War was declared on 3 September 1939, and shortly afterwards this recruiting advertisement appeared in the *Dudley Herald*. Young tradesmen were being asked to volunteer for the armed forces, who needed skilled engineering workers and builders. The volunteers would receive a craftsman's allowance on top of their ordinary pay. Those who were in reserved occupations or undertaking war work were asked not to volunteer, as they were already helping win the war by keeping industry going. On 1 October a royal proclamation was announced stating that all men aged twenty and twenty-one were to be called up. It was expected that 6,350 men would be affected in the Black Country.

HRH the Duke of Kent meeting members of the public in Dudley Market Place, *c.* 1940. It is believed that this visit took place when the Duke visited the Midlands on 19 December 1940, as part of his duties to visit war victims, the wounded and those who had been bombed. The *County Express* reported that for this visit his exact itinerary was not issued for security reasons, but that he inspected the Home Guard and met members of the public in Dudley Market Place after a visit to the Grace Mary Estate, Tividale, where he inspected recent bomb damage. The Duke was killed in an aeroplane crash in 1942 while on active duty with the RAF.

Inspection of civil defence services in the Market Place by HRH the Duke of Kent, 19 February 1941. Following a brief visit to Brierley Hill, the Duke of Kent accompanied by the Earl of Dudley arrived at Dudley Market Place where he was met by the mayor. The market stalls had been removed and civil defence personnel (including the Home Guard and ARP services) and vehicles were lined up for inspection. The Duke was presented to the heads of each service and he spent time talking to the men and women in the ranks, asking particularly about length of service and action seen. He was most impressed by the newly inaugurated civil defence cadets, brainchild of Alderman A.L. Hillman, first of a new service that it was hoped would spread nationwide.

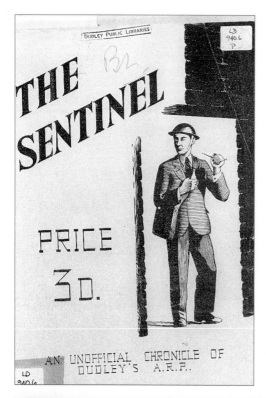

Front cover of *The Sentinel*, unofficial chronicle of Dudley's ARP, January 1940. This magazine, with a circulation of about a thousand, was edited and published by the Rev. C.G. Thompson of Darby End, head warden of ARP Group F. It received a hostile reception from the council who deemed its content to be too independent, irreverent and critical. They announced that no member of the ARP should write for *The Sentinel*, although when the publication was first mooted they had agreed that the ARP officer should contribute. This issue contained a rebuttal of the council's criticism, stating that the magazine was designed to inform the public of ARP developments, and to serve the movement. Any criticisms were to be seen as constructive and the ARP officer had approved the proofs before publication.

The mayoress, Mrs B.T. Horwood (centre), and a committee of ladies outside the Hippodrome Theatre, entertaining wounded soldiers, July 1940. The mayoress and her committee raised sufficient funds to enable groups of wounded soldiers recuperating in a local hospital to visit the theatre. On four consecutive Monday evenings between thirty and forty men were entertained to tea and taken to the Hippodrome, the Midland Red Bus Company supplying transport at a reduced cost. The group visiting the Hippodrome on Monday 15 July were introduced to Evelyn Laye, who was appearing at the theatre, and met them before the show. During the performance itself she came down into the audience and asked them to participate, which they did with gusto, singing along to a new song – 'Go to it'.

The committee that organised the Spitfire Fund, October 1940. Many towns were helping to raise money to buy Spitfires for the Air Force. It was felt that such a fund would appeal to Dudley people's imagination, and give them an opportunity to show their admiration for the RAF. So, at a public meeting on 23 August the Mayor of Dudley's Spitfire Fund was inaugurated, and a committee was duly formed to organise fund raising activities, the members being the mayor (Alderman B.T. Horwood), Ald J.H. Molyneux, Councillors Hillman, Butler and Moss, and Messrs Marsh, Wesley, Braithwaite, Fellows and Kennedy. Activities included house to house collections, auctions and competitions, and concluded with an intensive week of events from 7 to 14 October, culminating with a concert at the Hippodrome.

A captured German Messerschmitt displayed in the Council House courtyard from 8 October 1940. Large crowds came to see this, and for 6d visitors could have a seat in the cockpit. Proceeds went to the Spitfire Fund. Henry Hall, the dance band leader, is seen here climbing into the plane. The committee's final meeting was on 31 October, when the chairman thanked the townspeople for their generosity, and the committee members, especially the Kennedy brothers, who had arranged and met the costs of an all star concert which had been a huge success. It was attended by the Earl of Dudley, and Flanagan and Allan had topped the bill. The fund was closed on 2 November: it had raised £7,400, enough for one and a half Spitfires.

Satirical adverts for the Shropshire, Worcestershire and Staffordshire Electric Power Co., taken from the *Dudley Herald*, 24 January and 21 February 1942. The SWS was one of two companies supplying electricity to Dudley at this time, from its generating station on the banks of the River Stour, its head office being in Mucklow Hill, Halesowen. When the electricity industry was nationalised on 1 April 1948 the SWS was incorporated into the Midlands Electricity Board, which covered over a million consumers throughout the Black Country and the Potteries.

Anti-gas warfare squad, outside Lister Road council depot, *c.* 1941. The ARP formed decontamination squads in case the enemy should spray gas from the air or drop bombs containing gas. The sanitation department vehicles were to be used in removing gas deposits from streets, buildings and clothing. Anti-gas courses were run from June 1939 and 100 men were allocated to the squads, who wore protective suits of rubber and oilskin. Left to right are -?-, George Cadman, Samuel Healey, Harry Madelin, Jack Hadlington, -?-, Jim Timmins. The depot was used by the ARP during the war, while the garage opposite housed ambulances. The room on the extreme right was used for fumigation of bedding after notification of infectious diseases.

Dudley Home Guard camp at Kinver, *c.* 1942. The soldiers are seen here relaxing with a pint of beer. Initially the volunteers only received arm bands stencilled with LDV (Local Defence Volunteer) until enough khaki denim two-piece overalls could be manufactured. Members of the public were asked to hand in any shotguns or rifles for distribution to the LDV, and the men had to drill with sticks or garden tools until rifles could be supplied. The force was not intended for serious offensive fighting, but to hinder the enemy, and was nicknamed 'look, duck and vanish', though later they were instructed to delay the enemy by any means possible. By July the term Home Guard was in common usage: Churchill felt it more inspiring than LDV.

Dudley Home Guard in Grange Park, *c.* 1940. There had been a long tradition of amateur military forces in England, citizens being obliged to serve in militias when called upon. This culminated in the creation of the Territorial Army and the Home Guard. Churchill had advocated the creation of a Home Guard of men aged 40-plus in October 1939, but it was not until May 1940, when the predicted mass aerial bombardment feared did not materialise and the threat of invasion re-surfaced, that the Government announced the creation of a local defence force to be made up of ordinary citizens. They would not be paid, but would receive uniforms and arms. Over 500 men registered in Dudley during the first week.

The King and Queen inspecting Dudley's Girl Cadets, 26 February 1942. Over 10,000 people watched the King and Queen inspect 2,000 civil defence personnel on the Dudley county cricket ground, during a two-day visit to the Midlands. Their route from Darlaston via Tipton was lined with spectators including more than 6,000 children. The Queen was presented with a bouquet of daffodils by Enid Tromans on behalf of the children. The royal couple were very impressed by the uniforms of both the ambulance drivers and the cadets, the Queen commenting on how 'smart' and 'practicable' their slacks were; she was very smartly dressed in a grey ensemble. When the King and Queen finally left the grounds to go to Dudley station, three resounding cheers rang out.

Dudley Girls' High School harvest camp, 1942. Based at Dunchurch Hall School, Rugby, the girls worked on several farms throughout this area, stooking wheat, pitching and carting grain, feeding the animals and driving tractors. The girls had to send home for gloves because of problems with thistles. The harvest camp scheme, which had been in operation since June 1939, allowed schoolchildren to assist farmers who were short of labour in potato planting, fruit picking, harvesting corn and other seasonal jobs. The girls' camps of 1942 were reported to have been very successful, and the minister of agriculture and fisheries congratulated all head teachers on the contributions made by their pupils to the country's food production: 31,000 schoolchildren had put in 2.5 million hours of work.

Dudley Grammar School harvest camp at Burcot, July and August 1944. Before 1940 the school had organised a camp at the end of the summer which had provided a cheap holiday for the senior boys, but in 1940 farmers appealed for help during harvest time because of a labour shortage. Under the direction of the Worcester war agricultural committee the boys worked at George Bros's fruit farm at Evesham in 1940 and then from 1941 at Burcot Farm, Tardebigge. In 1944 two camps were held, sixty boys in each party – one in July during which the weather was splendid, the second in August when the weather was appalling. Between 10 and 15 tons of apples were picked each day, but much of the fruit was under-ripe.

Parade of Dudley trainee airmen, 346 ATC Squadron, at RAF Cosford during a Midland Command get together, *c.* 1943–44. The squadron is led by its CO, Flt Lt Bob Kennedy (proprietor of Dudley Hippodrome), and bringing up the rear is Flt Lt Matthews, his eventual successor. The airman pictured fourth from the right is Clarry Fenton; also seen are Des Boothby, Johnny Simpson, ? Robinson, Fred Lloyd, Ray Flanagan, Ivan Walker, Jack Hickman, ? Horton, Paul Fenton, Tommy Tipper, Derek Tipper, 'Ace' Hayward and ? McNaney. The Air Training Corps was established to provide sixteen to eighteen year old youths with pre-service training for the RAF, and the Dudley branch was founded on 21 January 1941. The dedication of their colours took place at St James's church, Dudley, on 14 February 1943.

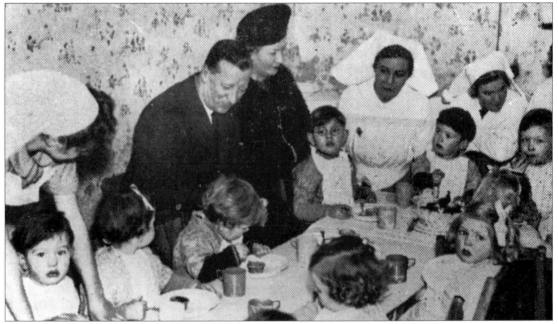

The mayor and mayoress attending a Christmas party at the Dixons Green wartime nursery, 21 December 1942. Wartime nurseries were developed in Dudley as an integral part of the war effort, as they enabled married women undertaking war work to leave their children to eat, sleep and play. Children were taken from a few months old up to the age of five and trained staff would look after their needs. A charge of 1s per day was made, but this included three meals a day, clothing and twelve hours of care. Dixons Green nursery had been a large house, and was extensively altered to accommodate up to forty children. Later nurseries at Limes Road and Netherton Park were purpose built.

The CWS National Works Fire Brigade, 1944. In common with many other industrial organisations, CWS in Hall Street formed their own fire brigade at this time. The work was part-time and drills and practice were done after hours. Captained by Arnold Craggs, the CWS team competed in the National Fire Service annual competitions and the group participated in the area finals at the Revo sports centre on 8 July 1944 after winning the Dudley divisional competition in the light trailer pump competition. Seen here is the winning team, with the cup. Back row, left to right: Capt. A. Craggs, Officers J. Gews, Smith, Parkes, L. Cox, Morris, W. Hayes, Gordon. Seated S. Sproston, H. Darby, C. Lloyd, J. Brough.

The disbandment of the Home Guard outside St Thomas's church, 3 December 1944. On a cold, grey, windy December day, Dudley's Home Guard was stood down. Despite a constant drizzle, the imposing ceremony in the Market Place was watched by hundreds of people who had gathered in the streets. The drab khaki battledress and steel helmets were relieved only by the colour of the mayoral robes. Since its inception over 3,500 men had enrolled with the Home Guard and the mayor thanked them all on behalf of the borough for their courage in being prepared to meet any emergency. Their final act was to take the royal salute, then the union jack and battalion colours were hoisted, and while the national anthem was played the company marched past before dispersing.

A street party during peace with victory celebrations, 7 June 1946. The mayor and mayoress are seen here serving ice cream to schoolchildren at Park Hill Junior School, during their tour of the borough's schools. School kitchen staff served tea to 10,000 schoolchildren altogether. Poor weather affected attendance at Saturday events, with many street parties being cancelled, bands rained off in Market Place, Netherton Park and Woodside Park and fêtes cancelled; only the indoor events were not affected adversely. During the evening the weather improved and the victory carnival dance was well attended. The climax of the events took place in a floodlit Market Place, where revellers gathered to dance once the streets were closed. Public buildings were floodlit, capturing the mood of the occasion.

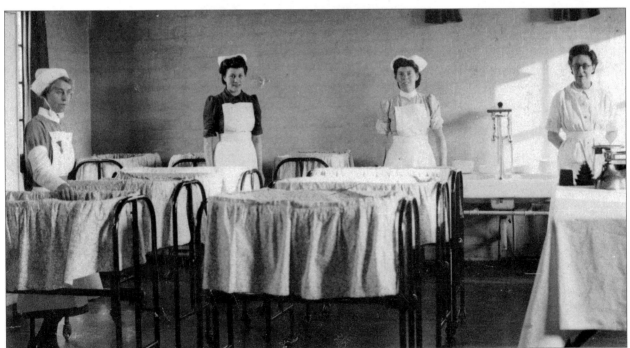

Rosemary Ednam Nursing Home, after 1945. Named after Rosemary, Viscountess Ednam who laid the foundation stone in 1926, and who died in an aeroplane crash on 21 July 1930, this nurses' and maternity home, known as Burton House, was erected under the aegis of the Dudley Board of Guardians and was officially opened on 11 September 1929 by Lady Harroby. The maternity home was a one-storey building and accommodated 11 beds within three wards. Under the Local Government Act, 1929, running of the nursing home became the responsibility of Staffordshire County Council, and two beds were reserved for Dudley cases. In 1947 there were 230 births at Rosemary Ednam Home, as Dudley Corporation rented additional beds.

Opening of the first postwar house, at Holly Hall, by the mayor, Alderman T.E. Bennett, July 1946. The mayor received the keys of the first of two permanent houses built for the corporation from Mr Beddall (of Batham & Beddall) and is seen here performing the opening ceremony, accompanied by the deputy mayor, the housing committee chairman and chief officials. The houses at Wood Street, Woodside, costing £1,100 each, were the first of twenty-eight being built by Batham & Beddall of Brierley Hill. A further twenty were built in the same area by another company. Housing was seen as a priority, with over three hundred families still living in what were categorised as slums.

Fourteen squatter families set up a new community in a former army camp, 15 August 1946. Rosemary Crescent was the name given by these families to the vacant accommodation they took over on the former American army camp off Burton Road. The first families to move in were the Batterbees, Goslings, Lanes and Jacksons, who were tired of waiting for decent homes. The occupation was done on the spur of the moment, but within twenty-four hours water and electricity supplies had been connected, official approval granted by Alderman Molyneux, the housing committee chairman and the chief sanitary officer, and a nominal rent decided upon. A squatter said: 'with the help of the council we can carry out their plan – homes fit for heroes'.

Hans Fiebusch working on the town hall mural, February 1948. Fiebusch is seen here preparing a tracing for the 25 ft long mural before starting to paint. In order to get the right perspective, the figures had to be sketched out, full scale, in the studio before being transferred on to the wall. The mural depicts Roger de Somery stag hunting in Kinver forest, and being held up by the King's men. The huntsmen were based on portraits of Alderman T.E. Bennett, A.V. Williams (town clerk), F.H. Gibbons (borough engineer) and C.V. Mackenzie (curator of the museum and art gallery).

Rock-making at Teddy Gray's, 1948. Famous for its lettered rock and herbal tablets, this business originated in 1826 when John Gray travelled the area selling home-made sweets. Gray's were one of the first rock-makers to introduce a picture design in the rock, marking Baden Powell's achievements in the Boer War. During the Second World War Gray's overseas trade was hit by rationing, as rock is made of sugar and glucose. Rock-making was still carried out by hand and J. Gray is seen here pulling out the large stick to the required size. With twenty-seven years' experience in the trade, Mr Gray had made over 2,000 tons of rock. The largest stick made in Dudley weighed 170 lb, and was raffled to raise funds for the Guest Hospital.

Mr. F.T. Tarry, HM Inspector of Constabulary, inspects the Dudley Police Force on the forecourt at Dudley Technical College, 19 August 1948. This was the first time that women police had appeared on the annual government inspectors' parade in Dudley. The Inspector spoke to all the constables, and he is seen here talking to WPC Ross, one of the policewomen. Also in the picture are the mayor, Councillor R. Little, Inspector J.T. Lloyd and the chief constable. Dudley's first two policewomen were appointed on 9 August 1947 and, according to the chief constable, it was hoped that their presence on the force would enable police to deal with young girls who were 'exposed to moral danger or beyond control'.

Market Place, 29 March 1949. The opening of Dudley's first zebra crossing by the mayor, Councillor R. Little, took place on Sunday 2 April at the start of a nationwide pedestrian crossing week. The new crossing was painted with yellow stripes in order to attract attention. During the week motorists were asked to be vigilant near all crossings, and pedestrians were asked to use them wherever possible. During January road safety exhibitions were held at Netherton Arts Centre and Dudley Town Hall; over 25,000 people were reported to have attended, including 9,000 schoolchildren. The aims of these events were to reduce road accidents and stop complacency. During 1949, 472 road accidents took place, including 6 fatal and 132 where injuries occurred, 55 more than the previous year – although 128 were attributed to dogs on the road.

CONCENTRATED CONSERVATISM!

LET DUDLEY

BE GOVERNED FROM ➤ DUDLEY AND NOT BY ▼

DUDLEY COUNCIL HOUSE

THE MAN FROM THE MINISTRY

YOUR LOCAL COUNCILLOR

INCHING ALL THE PAVEMENT

We were a Progressive Town up to 1945!! LET US FACE THE FACTS!!!

Front cover of the election campaign leaflet of Charles Rupert Newns, Conservative candidate for Netherton ward, 1949. This was the second time Mr Newns had stood as candidate. At the previous election he had been narrowly defeated by the defending candidate Alderman Tom Taylor, a sheetmetal worker who had represented Netherton for eight years. In these municipal elections of May 1949 the Labour party were at a disadvantage: of ten retiring councillors nine were Labour, three further seats had been created by ward changes, and the Conservatives were contesting each one. The Conservative party won overall control of the council by a narrow margin (seventeen seats to sixteen), but Mr Newns lost to Tom Taylor by 995 votes to 1,243.

Meena, Dudley Zoo's elephant, is weighed on the public weighbridge at Stone Street, 9 August 1949. These pictures appeared in the *Dudley Herald*, under the headline 'Meena puts on weight'. Dudley Zoo's elephant keeper was Mr G. Bates; he was in sole charge of the elephants from his arrival in 1937 until his death in November 1952. After the war the zoo's animal stocks were low. Its postwar recovery was generated by the new general manager Donald Bowles, an honours graduate in zoology and botany from Bristol University, who instigated the development of the grounds as well as dramatically increasing the animal stock. By 1949, when Bowles announced his resignation to go to Edinburgh Zoo, Dudley had one of the best stocked zoos in the country.

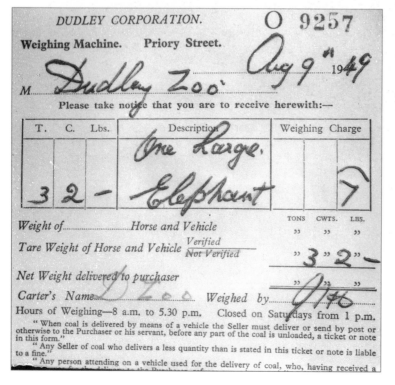

Weighing machine ticket for Meena the elephant, 1949. The weighbridge office originally stood in the Market Place, but it was later moved to Priory Street. In 1965 Councillor J.G. Rowley referred to it as 'an eyesore and white elephant'; maintenance was costly and takings were low. By 1966 a public weighbridge was already available at The Leys, Brockmoor, and a modern weighbridge was planned at the corporation depot at Lister Road. In February 1967 the office was dismantled and taken to storage, before being rebuilt at the Black Country Museum, as it was considered to be a good example of Victorian ironwork. The weighbridge had been little used for a number of years: in the month before demolition the takings only amounted to 14s 4d.

5. From Austerity to Affluence: the 1950s

Dudley schoolboy Duncan Edwards, picked for England, March 1950. The thirteen-year-old schoolboy is pictured here with his fellow pupils from Wolverhampton Street School. The boy on Duncan's right is Raymond Wooldridge, the school team's centre-half and grandson of Willy Wooldridge, a former captain of Wolverhampton Wanderers. Duncan loved football, playing for his school teams at Priory Road Junior School and Wolverhampton Street Schools. He was also chosen for the Dudley Boys, the Worcester County XI and finally the under-14 England Schoolboys against competition from older boys. Duncan's first match was against Ireland on 6 June 1950, the same day that he was to have appeared for his school at a folk-dancing festival in Derby.

Introduction

The 1950s probably saw some of the biggest changes of the century in the lives of ordinary people. Great strides had been taken by the government after the war to eliminate hardship caused by poverty, especially of the old and the sick, by the creation of the welfare state, which provided sickness and unemployment benefit, pensions and family allowances. In 1950 shortages were the norm, but living standards gradually improved, and unemployment stayed low so people prospered. The problem of slum housing was being tackled, with the building of council accommodation, and environmental conditions improved after the Clean Air Act was passed in 1956. By the end of the decade Harold Macmillan said that 'most of our people have never had it so good'.

The postwar Labour government presided over shortages, rationing, high prices and high taxes. The NHS ran into financial difficulties almost immediately, so the government introduced charges for prescriptions, some dental treatment and spectacles. Defence spending increased when a two-year National Service scheme was introduced, leading to less money for hospitals and houses. Inflation led to price increases, then workers demanded higher wages fuelling further inflation; many people emigrated at this time. In the 1951 election the Conservatives led by Churchill were returned to power.

The working environment was dramatically changed by technology; the introduction of mechanical aids such as forklift trucks, hoists and bulldozers meant that less physical effort was required in many jobs. Labour shortages in transport and nursing led to increasing immigration from Africa, Asia and the West Indies. The immigrants worked hard and saved to bring their families to live in Britain, but many faced racism, particularly when trying to find housing. Dudley was no exception to this.

Technological progress was made in the fields of power, medicine and transport. The first nuclear power station was opened in 1956, to provide energy without using fossil fuels. The first vaccinations against polio were given, and the government took action to stop smog being created in the cities and towns. Road safety was improved, and in 1959 the first motorway was opened from London to the north.

As the population grew throughout the 1950s, so did the demand for decent housing. Army barracks were pressed into service, prefabricated houses built and a massive programme of council house building started. People looked forward to increasing prosperity, food rationing ceased and technological advances were made, creating affordable household appliances which certainly made life easier and more enjoyable – in particular washing machines, vacuum cleaners, telephones, radios and refrigerators. Television became more widely available, and rapidly became a focal point in the home. Television licence holders increased dramatically from 3,248 in 1954 to 7 million in

1957. In Dudley, as in many other places, the funeral of King George VI and the coronation of Elizabeth II were watched on television. There was also an increase in private car ownership. Hire purchase schemes proliferated, making these consumer goods more affordable by spreading the payments.

Family life was changing. Before the war the father was the breadwinner and his wife stayed at home to look after the house and their children. Upon marriage many women, even in the professions – for example civil servants, teachers and librarians – lost their jobs. During the war women had been needed in the workplace; afterwards their contribution was still required to boost production, so many stayed at work. This helped increase standards of living and provided fulfilment for many.

Improvements were made in education, with the introduction of nursery schools and free secondary schools for all children aged eleven to fifteen. For the first time in history young people had money to spend on fast food, entertainment and clothes, and a separate youth culture began to develop. Rebellious teenagers began to develop their own ideas and style rather than conform to the dictates of behaviour laid down by their parents, and expressed their views vigorously. Their tastes in fashion and music at times shocked their elders.

The music industry was dominated at the start of the '50s by crooners and the big bands. Country music, jazz and the blues were becoming more popular and would later influence pop music. A particularly British phenomenon was the skiffle band, teenagers forming a group to play music on guitars and instruments made from household objects, especially washboards. Rock and roll reached Britain in 1955, when teenagers were to shock their elders by jiving in the aisles at Bill Haley films.

The typical early '50s look for girls was that of a tight-waisted swinging skirt worn over several petticoats, with a wide belt and shirt-style blouse, hair often tied in a ponytail, sometimes with an alice-band. By 1958 the backcombed 'beehive' hairdo had developed, and girls were wearing print dresses, nylons, high heeled shoes and matching nail varnish and lipstick. By 1955 boys were rebelling against their staid clothes, and started wearing Edwardian-style long jackets, drainpipe trousers and bootlace ties; they grew their hair and sideburns, greased their hair and teased it into quiffs. They became known as 'Teddy Boys'.

There was an upsurge in leisure pursuits now that people had much more free time, because of the shorter working week and increased holiday entitlement. In 1951 the Festival of Britain took place: it was intended to boost trade and people's spirits after the bleakness of war. Football was a big spectator sport, and there was enormous sorrow at the 1959 Munich air disaster which killed seven members of the Manchester United football team, including Dudley's famous son Duncan Edwards. There were no purpose-built leisure centres or health clubs, and young people gathered in coffee bars with jukeboxes, often forming music and dancing clubs. With the development of jet travel foreign holidays became more widely available, but most people still travelled by rail or bus to the seaside for their holidays. Holiday camps became very popular during the '50s.

Flooding at Netherton, 1950. At teatime on Wednesday 7 June a freak storm hit Dudley and over half an inch of rain fell in 45 minutes; for about 15 minutes hailstones measuring half an inch across thundered down. Many roads in low lying areas were flooded, holding up traffic. In Netherton, St Peter's Road was flooded up to a depth of 2 ft, and the families living at 41–2 St Thomas's Road were very badly hit when rain poured through their roofs, soaking their beds and then rushing down the stairs. The mayor, on seeing the devastated families clearing up by candlelight with their sodden bedclothes in the street, promised council help. Elsewhere, chimneys were struck by lightning, with manhole covers and road surfaces being forced up and broken.

Building the war memorial swimming baths, Dudley Grammar School, spring 1950. Over 700 Old Boys of Dudley Grammar School served in the Second World War and forty-three lost their lives, so in March 1946 an appeal fund was launched. It was felt that a swimming pool in the school grounds would give pleasure to successive generations of pupils, and a memorial would be erected nearby as a permanent record of their sacrifice. The cost of £5,000 was met by subscriptions and fund-raising events. Work started in October 1949, the contractors being A.J. Crump & Sons, and the official opening was performed by the Bishop of Worcester on Saturday 24 June 1950. After the ceremony bereaved relatives placed wreaths on the tablet.

Mr Joe Perkins is pictured here working on his intricate models at his home at 33 Willow Road, Dudley, 25 August 1950. Joe made his first model, a boat, after the First World War and had now progressed to producing models of fairground machinery, some with over 3,000 parts. The piece he is working on here includes working swing boats, illumination and a hidden gramophone to provide the music. His favourite model was a working replica of a roundabout, which had been valued at £5 6s. Local children often visited Joe to watch the working models, and brought him scrap materials like wood, corks, tin or other metals for his current project.

Hop pickers, 6 September 1950. This photograph shows a typical party waiting outside the Wrens Nest public house on Priory Road for transport to what had become an annual event for many families. In the centre is Edward Mansell holding his son Michael and their terrier Pal. Hop pickers travelled to farms in Herefordshire and Worcestershire to help with the harvest for two to three weeks. Basic accommodation was usually provided, but families would take all the impediments needed for their daily lives. Mechanisation was being introduced in the form of McConnel Hinds mechanical picking machines to reduce costs, but there was still plenty of work in 1950 as only fifteen or twenty farmers in the Midlands had purchased machines.

Civil defence exercise, April 1951. Curious passers-by stop and look at the strange sight of a man dangling from a rope on the end of an extending ladder, high above a Dudley street. This incident was part of an exercise organised by the civil defence to simulate a rescue operation following an aeroplane crash on the roof which had set the building alight, trapping people on the top floor. The fire brigade and civil defence workers summoned by the sirens arrived and performed a rescue. The watching crowd was told by the authorities that had this been an actual rescue, not an exercise, then lives would have been lost owing to the shortage of civil defence volunteers.

Dudley Wood clinic, c. 1952. After numerous delays this long-needed £14,000 clinic was opened on 20 February 1952 by Alderman A.E. Young. His father, the late Councillor Alex Young, had been instrumental in its inception and his son, Alan, was selected to be the architect. The builders of this single-storey clinic were A.J. Crump & Sons of Aston Road. The clinic was set in ⅛ acre of ground, the garden layout being funded by a bequest from Alex Young. It could not initially offer a full service, because of a shortage of staff as a result of the borough's dispute with the BMA over salary scales for medical officers of health, but it would eventually fulfil the borough's maternity and child welfare requirements.

Choral and Orchestral Festival, 1951. A choir of over 700 children and an orchestra of thirty, representing secondary schools in south-west Staffordshire, filled the stage and the bulk of the floor space of the town hall at this music festival. The programme concentrated on English music, from the earliest written music to the present day, and works by Midlands composers Elgar (Worcestershire), Vaughan Williams and Gustav Holst (Gloucestershire) were performed. Vaughan Williams composed the piece 'Flourish the trumpet' especially for the festival. Although an ambitious programme, it was an impressive performance and there were some rich harmonies. Dudley's celebrations during Festival Year centred around the Dudley Pageant, a re-enactment of historical events and community life through the ages.

Birmingham Road and Castle Hill, 1952. This shot was taken before the improvements at Tipton Road. Reconstruction of this area started in 1949 with the conversion of part of Birmingham Road from single to dual carriageway. It was made of reinforced concrete with centre islands, new footpaths were laid out and a new lighting system was installed. Plans were also made to reconstruct Tipton Road from its junction with Station Bridge to the railway goods yard, and work began on this in 1950. It had been hoped to convert it to a dual carriageway the following year, but this did not happen until 1953, by which time it had become an accident blackspot and safety had become a big issue.

Pupils at Jessons Junior Mixed School about to watch the king's funeral, 15 February 1952. Following the death of George VI on 6 February, Elizabeth was proclaimed queen on 8 February. The children listened to the events at school on the radio, although the headmistress allowed some children to go home to watch them on television. She hired a television from the MEB so that all the children could watch the king's funeral: it was placed in the school hall so school meals on that day were eaten in the classrooms. At 2 p.m. everyone stood for the two minutes silence and then watched the service. In town, shops closed before the two minutes silence, reopening later. The market remained open, but little business took place.

Parishioners at St John's church watching the king's funeral on four borrowed television sets – also from the MEB, 1952. The sets were installed the previous day and the vicar, Rev. H.E. Jones, stayed in church overnight in case of burglary or vandalism. Admission was by ticket only so that the atmosphere would remain devout. Sixty-three parishioners witnessed the funeral, and later 120 more arrived and listened to the continued sound coverage. There were also memorial services at St Thomas's and St Edmund's churches at 1.30 p.m., attended by local businessmen and office staff. In town the two minutes silence was signalled by the firing of a warning rocket: even traffic came to a halt.

Mrs Pole making handbags for HRH Queen Elizabeth, the Queen Mother, 27 February 1952. The royal family attended the British Industries Fair at Earls Court in 1951, where they visited the stand of leather goods manufacturer, John Douglas & Sons, a subsidiary of J. & A. Hillman Ltd who produced fancy leather and sports goods. They were greeted at the stand by Mr Arthur Hillman, company director. The then queen ordered three handbags, two in calf (one black and one navy) and one in gabardine (red). Apparently this was the sixth successive time that the queen had placed an order at the BIF. In 1949 the royal family had placed an order for eighteen items.

Snow clearing, New Street, 1952. This was a typical scene on Monday 30 March: shopkeepers and staff are pictured here clearing the snow and slush from the pavements in front of their shops before starting their normal business. High winds on Friday and Saturday from Russia and heavy snowfall on Saturday brought blizzard conditions over the weekend with drifts about 4 in deep. Records show that this was the coldest March for eighty-one years. The horse drawn Co-op delivery van, on the far side of the road, was still a familiar sight in the Midlands in the 1950s.

Liberal walking party, Castle Street, 22 September 1952. Six university undergraduates from Oxford, Cambridge and London universities aimed to put forward the Liberal party's point of view, to attack the government and to criticise both Tory and Socialist policies. They styled themselves the 'Commandos' and conducted their offensive by using sandwich boards, leaflets, handbells and loudspeakers. The group spent a week in the Midlands, spreading their message by holding impromptu meetings in town centres and visiting factories. Their aim was to return enough Liberal representatives at the next election so that, in their view, the new government would be in the best interests of the people.

St Edmund's church, 24 April 1953. R.T. Barratt, keeper of the public clocks, is shown here repairing the church clock. He replaced one of the hands on the dial facing Dudley station, and synchronised all three dials. The Dudley Fire Brigade provided assistance in the form of a turntable ladder. Passers-by seemed unconcerned, carrying on with their daily business. Later that year, after a wooden louvre crashed into the street narrowly missing a car, an inspection found the tower to be unsafe. Immediate renovations were required in the form of replacement louvres and tower floorboards. A bazaar was held to raise money for the repairs, £524 being collected.

Market Place coronation celebrations, Tuesday 2 June 1953. Thousands attended these events, despite the gloomy weather. The day of the coronation was cold, wet and windy, but most events planned went ahead. Market Place was closed to traffic so open-air dancing could take place; and although the crowd was reluctant to take part initially, by 3 p.m. a party of girls were dancing in the square. The rain stopped later and by 11 p.m. the Market Place was filled with hundreds of people, many wearing paper hats, dancing the waltz, foxtrot and jitterbug. Officially arranged to cease at midnight, the dancing went on until after 1 a.m. Police kept a benevolent eye on the proceedings but there was no trouble.

Other events in Dudley included a PT display by the Women's Junior Air Corps and a continuity drill by the ATC at the sports centre. Planned firework displays were cancelled, but bonfires were lit at Shavers End, Cawney Hill and Netherton. A brazier was lit at the castle but it went out because of high winds and rain. Many areas held street parties and schools distributed souvenirs. During the week preceding the coronation, the municipal offices, priory ruins and Netherton church were all floodlit, and the corporation ran a best decorated street and shop competition. Dingle Road, Oakham, won the prize for best street and Mrs A. Harper, florist of 174 Wolverhampton Street, won the prize for best decorated shop.

St James's Road, 18 November 1953. 'Bandits in St James's Road?': so started the *Dudley Herald*'s article on 21 November. The man illustrated here was actually testing a smog mask, to the apparent amusement of passers-by. The health minister, Iain McLeod, had just announced that doctors could prescribe these masks on the NHS to patients most likely to be affected by pollution. Smog, a combination of intense fog, smoke and cold, could be dangerous to people with heart or lung diseases; until air pollution could be eliminated these masks were considered the best way to minimise risks. The Clean Air Act of 1956 gave local authorities the right to control smoke emissions, and Russells Hall estate was created Dudley's first smokeless zone.

Dudley Wood, 1954. On 14 June heavy rainstorms caused major flooding in the Dudley Wood area. Torrential rain caused the water level in Mousesweet Brook, a tributary of the River Stour marking the boundary between Dudley and Rowley Regis, to rise above the bridge very quickly. Lakes about 50 ft in diameter formed on both sides of the bridge causing traffic to Cradley to be diverted. The Rev. Frank Binns, the vicar of St John's church, was most concerned as the foundation stone for the new church hall, just 20 yds from the brook, had only been laid the preceding Saturday. The waters reached within 10 ft of the workings before subsiding.

Bowling Green County Junior Mixed School, Exeter Road, Netherton, 16 March 1954. This school was built to alleviate overcrowding at three local schools. Re-organisation brought together the junior departments from Dudley Wood Junior and Infants, Halesowen Road Junior and Infants and Halesowen Road Mixed schools. The building was designed by J.T. Lewis, the borough architect, and built by B. Whitehouse & Sons at a cost of £111,000. It had a number of special features including a self-contained dining room, seen here: the children are queuing for their meal. There was also a spacious assembly hall, eleven form rooms and two large additional general purpose classrooms. The official opening was performed by George Wigg, Dudley's MP, on 26 March 1954.

Broadway Hall seen here in the process of construction, 2 October 1954. This imposing four-storey hall of residence for Dudley Training College was designed by architect Alan Young, and built by George Webb & Sons of Birmingham at a cost of £65,000 to house sixty-three women students. There were twenty-one bedrooms on each of the three upper floors with the communal areas on the ground floor. It was needed as the college was attracting students from all over the country, numbers having risen from 140 after the war to 213 in 1954. Total student accommodation, once Broadway Hall was open, was 105 men and 113 women. It was officially opened by S.F. Burman, vice-chancellor of Birmingham University, on 17 March 1956.

Twelve people, including five young children and one baby were hurt in this bus crash at Marriott Road, Netherton, 12 May 1956. The victims were taken to the Guest Hospital for treatment, but there were no serious injuries, the worst being a broken collar bone, and all were allowed home after treatment. Apparently the driver of a Midland Red double-decker bus lost control on a steep section of road; the bus hit a wall and overturned. Residents rushed to help as the passengers escaped through the upstairs emergency and rear exits. An eyewitness, Harry Homer, was only 30 yds from the accident and helped with the rescue. The Dudley students' carnival procession was held up while ambulances and police rushed to the incident.

The Gipsies Tent public house, 3 October 1956. Bert Millard and his father Harry are seen here relaxing with a cup of tea after an early start. Harry had been stoking the boiler, while Bert had been cleaning out the fermentation vessels, preparing to make their home-brew ale. The Millard family had owned the pub since about 1867, when George Millard had stopped in Dudley en route to America and spotted the pub for sale. Brewing ceased in 1961 when threatened compulsory purchase made investment in new equipment pointless. The pub closed in 1980 when Bert and his brother retired, but it is still standing. Originally called the Jolly Collier, it was renamed in the 1870s, its name inspired by a nearby gipsies' settlement.

The visit of Their Royal Highnesses Queen Elizabeth II and Prince Philip, 23 April 1957. This was part of a tour covering eleven towns in the Midlands. The royal party were met at the Dudley boundary at Burnt Tree by the mayor and mayoress together with the town clerk and the chief constable. Cheering crowds lined the route into Dudley along Birmingham Road and Castle Hill to the Broadway, where many people had arrived early to establish a good view. The photograph above shows the Queen in the Civic Gardens, acknowledging the cheers of about five thousand schoolchildren; the lower one shows her being warmly applauded by the crowd as she walks along Priory Road with the mayor, Councillor S. Danks. This was the couple's first visit to Dudley, which had been colourfully decorated for the occasion. Following the presentation of a bouquet in Coronation Gardens, by Penelope Joy Roberts, the royal party walked to the town hall steps where they greeted about fifty local dignitaries. After lunch the Queen was presented with a leather handbag and the Duke of Edinburgh with a leather portrait folder made by a local firm. As they left Dudley en route to Brierley Hill, via Priory Road, Castle Street and High Street, the bells of St Thomas's pealed out.

Saturday night dance at the town hall, 1956. This was a popular meeting place for young people. Music was usually performed live by a dance band: Styx Williams and his broadcasting band are seen here. The dances often included ballroom dances; however, young people adopted the 'jive' (as illustrated in this photograph) and would dance it at any opportunity, to any music with the appropriate beat. Teenagers, especially girls, were fashion conscious and most of the girls seen here were wearing the tight-waisted, circular full skirt and shirt-style blouse that were popular at the time, while the boys wore the standard smart suit with a tie, or sports jacket with dark trousers.

Detectives investigating the murder of David Keasey in 1957. Detective Superintendent G. Millar of Scotland Yard and Detective Constable G. Moffat of Dudley CID are seen here outside the alley leading to the side entrance of Halford's men's outfitters where twenty-one-year-old David Alan Keasey was found shot on Friday 17 May. Dennis Howard was arrested on 22 June and confessed to the killing, but at his trial on 17 October he pleaded not guilty, saying that he took the gun merely to frighten Keasey, and that it went off by accident in a struggle. He was found guilty and sentenced to death. Following a failed appeal, Howard was hanged at Winson Green Prison on 4 December.

The jazz club at the Hen and Chickens, seen here at what was probably its inaugural session on 27 February 1958. Denis Sury, leader of the March Hares jazz band, was instrumental in setting up the club, which met each Thursday at the Hen and Chickens between 8 and 10.30 p.m. Only three weeks after formation the club boasted over 100 members, its success largely owing to its low annual subscription of 1s 6d, the gap in the teenage entertainment market and the popularity of the resident band, The March Hares, formed in 1957. They were a traditional jazz band, the only one of its type to include a flautist, with a wide repertoire, and had played with a number of distinguished jazz musicians. The group, shown in the photograph below, was made up of Johnny Walker (drums), Bill Griffiths (double bass), Bill Brown (trombone), Bob Ivan (trumpet), Trevor Orton (clarinet, saxophone and flute), Ray Aston (flute) and Graham Freeman (trombone). Their leader Denis Sury played the banjo and guitar. The group considered the Hen and Chickens the best venue to play in the Midlands and hoped that the club might reach capacity at 150 members. It attracted 'cats' from all over the Midlands to jive or just sit and listen to the music. The photograph on the right shows Terry Cashmore, complete with wellington boots, dancing with Wendy Epotts.

Bishop Milner Roman Catholic School, Burton Road, under construction, 1958. At the end of 1956 approval was given for the building of a new three-storey Roman Catholic Secondary school for 400 pupils, with a provision built in to cater for 600 in the future. The school was to be designed by the borough architect at an estimated cost of £191,000 and it would include a gymnasium, science and art rooms, a library and a large assembly hall with a stage at one end and an oratory at the other. Prior to building, though, the site had to be cleared and levelled, and it was not until June 1958 that the brickwork could be seen.

Bishop Milner Roman Catholic School, Burton Road, nearing completion, 1959. It was named after Bishop John Milner, the Vicar Apostolic of the Midlands who struggled for religious freedom for Catholics, and was a learned theologian and prolific writer. Although born in London, he attended Sedgley Park School from 1765 before training for the priesthood. He died in 1826 in Wolverhampton. When the school opened in January 1960, there were thirteen classes catering for 460 pupils, drawn from Dudley, Tipton, Oldbury, Sedgley and Brierley Hill. The official opening by the Most Rev. Francis Grimshaw, Archbishop of Birmingham, took place on 21 September 1960. In his speech Mr Eisel, Dudley's chief education officer, stressed the importance of the fourth 'R' in education – Religion.

Castle Scooter Club, 1 June 1958. The club was founded in 1957 and one year later its membership stood at thirty. Weekly meetings were held, usually at Midland Scooters Ltd, Castle Hill, but occasionally at other venues. The picture here is of a few members of the club relaxing with a game of rounders (the batsman is Patrick Burrows), during a weekend rally competition. The competition incorporated an 80-mile run to Ironbridge, and the scooters were subject to a stability test and a stringent hill test.

The post office, 141 Salop Street, *c.* 1959. Pictured here is Mr S. White, postmaster. This post office closed in March 1971, and its replacement opened across the road in West Street. Dudley Council purchased no. 141 and other properties in Salop Street for demolition, for the proposed road widening and landscaping for Dudley College of Education, which was carried out in the early '70s. Directories show that the Eve Hill sub-post office was at 12 Himley Road in about 1928, the postmaster being T.H.F. Evans, and transferred to 141 Salop Street in about 1930 under Albert H. Richards. Later postmasters included Edward C. Blackwell, Jos. Danks, ? Kilmster, John T. Brown and finally, from about 1954, Stanley White.

Duncan Edwards's funeral, 26 February 1958. This talented young man, the youngest ever player to have represented England at this time, had played football for his country eighteen times by the age of twenty-one and had been tipped as a possible successor to Billy Wright as captain. These moving pictures outside St Francis's church reflect the depth of feeling of Dudley's citizens when the Manchester United player died from the terrible injuries he sustained in the Munich air disaster. Over 2,000 people gathered outside the church and the short choral service conducted by the Rev. A. Dawson Catterall, was relayed to a packed church hall. Police had to keep the church entrance clear for the pallbearers, his England team-mates Billy Wright (Wolves), Ronnie Clayton (Blackburn Rovers), Don Howe and Ray Barlow (both West Bromwich Albion), Peter McFarland and Pat Saward (both Aston Villa), as people surged forward. There were over 300 wreaths and floral tributes sent from all over Europe, which filled the Edwards's front garden. After the service the funeral procession drove through the Market Place up High Street past St Thomas's church to the borough cemetery, many thousands of bare-headed mourners lining the route. As Duncan was buried, the vicar's words during the service, 'Go forward Duncan Edwards from this place rich in achievement, honoured and loved by us all – forward into the dawn', reflected the sentiments of the town.

6. The 1960s and 1970s

Birmingham Road, 1962. Tipton Road is on the left and Trindle Road on the right in the foreground. The shot seems to have been taken from the Station Hotel, and the Midland Red bus garage can be seen on the right. The Ministry of Transport had given approval for the traffic lights at the junction of Birmingham Road and Trindle Road in May 1962 in an attempt to reduce heavy traffic in High Street, and to encourage motorists to use the inner ring road, via King Street and Trindle Road. Today a traffic island stands at the bottom of Tipton Road, and the bus garage was demolished in 1994 to make way for the new Dudley Southern Bypass.

Introduction

The 1960s and 1970s were decades of great change in Britain, and Dudley was no exception. The '60s were the years of 'Swinging London' and the first incarnation of 'Cool Britannia'. Britain had emerged from the grey days of the immediate postwar period, and was riding a wave of optimism. Unemployment was low, at about 2 per cent, and pay was on the increase: the average national wage increased from £13 a week in 1961 to £23 a week in 1968. At the same time there seemed to be a surge in new creative talent, with young designers like Mary Quant in fashion, artists like David Hockney, and photographers such as David Bailey. Cities, many of which had been damaged by wartime bombing, were being rebuilt in glass, concrete and steel; slum housing was replaced by tower blocks, and new fabrics, such as perspex and coloured plastic, abounded in interior design. There was great confidence in all things new. This was the decade when the postwar 'baby boomers' became teenagers, and youth and novelty were to be celebrated. Fashions changed dramatically, for both men and women, and the British music scene was at its most vibrant. At the same time literary and theatre censorship were ended, and society seemed to become generally more free.

Greater affluence and modern throw-away materials also had a downside. Car ownership increased enormously, leading to congestion in town centres. Many new roads had to be built, including the motorway network, and older streets were widened to accommodate increased traffic. Some people, particularly the hippies, were beginning to warn of the effects on the ecology of the earth, and draw attention to pollution and the exploitation of natural resources. For Britain, too, it was a time of adjustment to a new world scene. The Empire had been dismantled, and yet Britain was denied entry to the EEC in 1963. This was also the nuclear age, and the threat of annihilation seemed very real at some times during the 1960s, leading to the establishment of CND.

In Dudley the local authority became involved in an ambitious redevelopment programme, demolishing much of the old town centre and continuing with the clearance of slum housing. Old shops were replaced by modern precincts and shopping centres, containing ambitious works of modern public art; roads were widened and pedestrianised; and dilapidated houses were replaced by comfortable modern housing estates and tower blocks. The face of Dudley, as of many towns, was changed forever.

The 1970s, by contrast, were years of unrest, high inflation and unemployment, and political instability in Britain. In 1970 more working days were lost through industrial action than in any year since the General Strike of 1926, and the government twice declared a state of emergency as a result of strikes. In 1972 the miners went on strike, and in 1974 the three-day week was introduced. Unemployment figures reached 1 million in 1972, for the first time since the war, and had risen to 1.3 million by the end of the decade. Taxes increased, with the introduction of VAT at 8 per cent in 1972, and its increase to 15 per cent in 1977. Inflation was a continual problem, and it reached a high of 36 per cent in June 1975.

Local government experienced changes after the Local Government Act of 1972, which, among other things, redrew many boundaries. The old Dudley county borough had already been expanded in 1966, to take in Brierley Hill and parts of Sedgley and Coseley, and in 1974 it took in Halesowen and Stourbridge also. The whole borough then found itself removed from its traditional county affiliations to Staffordshire and Worcestershire, and became part of the new West Midlands County Council.

Decimal currency, introduced in February 1971, was a big change for Britain and was intended to bring the country more into line with Europe. The Conservative and Liberal parties were generally in favour of joining the EEC, while Labour was generally against. Britain was finally accepted for membership, beginning in 1973. Once back in power, Labour held a referendum on whether Britain should stay in, and two-thirds of electors voted to do so.

Crime increased dramatically, by 50 per cent between 1973 and 1977 alone, and vandalism was costing millions of pounds. The high-rise flats, which had been greeted with such enthusiasm in the 1960s, came in for increasing criticism. In 1970 the NSPCC warned that living in flats could damage children's development, but by the end of the decade 300,000 children still lived in flats above the second floor.

There were steps forward, however. The women's liberation movement burst on to the scene, and women achieved many firsts during the decade, particularly in the field of employment. In 1975 the Sex Discrimination Act made it illegal to discriminate against women, and the Equal Opportunities Commission was established. The Race Relations Act of 1976 aimed to end discrimination against people on grounds of race. Technology was advancing, and many household appliances, such as fridges and washing machines, became more widely available. The Queen's silver jubilee in 1977 was celebrated across the nation, with royal visits and street parties.

Locally, the 1970s brought Dudley's first lady mayor, Dr Katherine Rogers, and the last days of selective education in the town, when the 400-year-old Grammar School went comprehensive. Redevelopment continued, including the new court buildings in the Inhedge. Council house tenants, with the support of some councillors, protested loud and long over increased rents as a result of the Housing Finance Act, and a new Socialist Tenants and Ratepayers party was established by Councillor Frank Hadden. These were turbulent times, and Dudley in 1979 was a very different place than it had been in 1960.

The mayor inspects the 7th Battalion Worcestershire Regiment, after the freedom of the borough ceremony, 8 April 1961. This honour was given to the Worcestershire Regiment 'in appreciation of their magnificent feats of arms, courage, sacrifice and devotion to duty' and because of their 'close association' with the borough, going back to 1881, when the Dudley Rifle Volunteers became part of the 1st Volunteer Battalion of the Worcestershire Regiment. The ceremony took place on Dudley Grammar School's sports ground, with the 1st and 7th battalions on parade. Afterwards the soldiers marched through the town, with 500 old comrades, led by Lt Col J. Parkes who commanded the 7th Battalion at Dunkirk. The regiment was presented with four silver bugles and an illuminated scroll.

The Staffordshire Regiment march past a saluting base in Market Place, after receiving the freedom of the borough from the mayor in Coronation Gardens, 29 April 1967. The Worcestershire Regiment had received the honour six years previously. This award to the Staffordshire Regiment reflects the boundary changes implemented in 1966. Dudley had always closely guarded its historic links with Worcestershire, but after 1966 the county borough included Brierley Hill, Kingswinford, Sedgley, Coseley and Wordsley, which had equally strong links with Staffordshire. In front of the platform can be seen several soldiers in 1705 uniforms, as this was the date of creation of the regiment. The borough presented eight trumpets and six fifes.

HRH Princess Margaret speaking to a Commonwealth student during her visit to Dudley Training College, 21 November 1962. The Princess and Lord Snowdon, her husband, officially opened the £400,000 extensions to the college. These included new halls of residence, and a new teaching wing, comprising a library, assembly hall for 600, and departments of art and crafts, religious education, geography, social studies, economics, commerce and history. Around fifteen thousand people lined the route to the Training College, including children from twenty-nine local schools. The Princess unveiled a plaque, gave a short speech, and was then taken on a tour of the extensions, where she met several students.

Race riots in Dudley, August 1962. Violence began on the evening of Monday 30 July, when around two hundred white people, carrying sticks, stones, iron bars, broken bottles and other weapons, marched on the North Street area of Dudley, where the town's ethnic minority population was then centred. Windows were smashed, and it was the early hours before the police managed to restore order. The police were out in force, along with five police dogs, brought in from Staffordshire and Wolverhampton. In total, fifty-eight people were arrested over three days. The authorities blamed boredom, following the beginning of the factory holidays, rather than racial prejudice for the rioting, but Dudley's 1,000-strong ethnic minority population were undoubtedly targeted.

The 3 Dees present a copy of their first single to the mayor, at Stanton's music shop, 4 May 1963, Dudley. Pictured, from left to right: Brian 'Don' Hudson, Roy Hiscox alias 'David Leigh', Frank Webb (the mayor) and John 'Dean' Hale. All of the band members were born in Dudley and were students at Dudley Grammar School and later the technical college. Their band became well known locally by playing in dance halls and clubs, and they moved to London in 1962 to pursue their musical career. Their first single was 'Well You Started It'. It sold well locally in its first week in the shops, but did not feature in the hit parade.

Workmen discover a sixteenth-century timber-framed building, while demolishing three shops in High Street, May 1963. The contractors employed to knock down shops in High Street, to allow for road widening, found half-timbered walls and wattle and daub panels behind the brick façade. Other finds included a wooden door with a spy hole, several old floorboards, and a headstone dated 1655. It was supposed that the building had once been a merchant's or tradesman's town house, and perhaps later had been used by a leather worker or shoe maker, who had apprentices living in. It seemed, though, that no-one was sufficiently interested to preserve the buildings, although the borough engineer did promise to investigate.

120

Wren's Nest Secondary Modern School nearing completion, April 1964. The children in the foreground are all from Priory Estate. Work began on the new secondary school in September 1963. It was intended as a replacement for the Wolverhampton Street Schools, which the local education authority wanted to close as soon as possible, to take some of the pressure off Park Schools. The school cost around a £250,000 to build, and would accommodate over 500 pupils. The building work was due to be completed by the summer of 1964; several delays occurred, however, and the first pupils were not admitted until May 1965. The school was officially opened by Lord Cobham on 15 October 1965.

Six Foot Road, Netherton, with flats in St John's Street under construction in the background, June 1965. Six Foot Road was included in the Dudley Corporation (St John's Street No. 2) (Netherton) Compulsory Purchase Order of 1956, but it took some time for all of the valuations and purchases to be settled. The old houses were mostly dark and damp with bad ventilation. They were badly arranged and most had fallen into disrepair. The inhabitants had to share yards and outside toilets, and some of the properties had no indoor water supply. The new flats and maisonettes on St John's Street were built by Wates (Midlands) Ltd at a cost of a little over £435,000.

Market Place, left, and Castle Street, below, 1965. The Chinese restaurant, whose sign is so prominent in the first picture, was the Chu Kong restaurant, which was at 248 Castle Street from the late 1950s through to the mid-1960s. It then briefly became the Seven Oceans, before the building was taken over by the MEB. It illustrates the wider range of foods, and the diversity of cultures, which were becoming part of postwar life in Britain. Next door was the Hen and Chickens, which became Cash Converters in 1995, and opposite (the curved building in the bottom picture) on the corner of Fisher Street is the Angel pub, later the Market Tavern. Traffic was permitted in Market Place at all times until 1973, when pedestrianisation was introduced on a trial basis, on Saturdays only. There were some initial worries about increasing traffic elsewhere, the effect on trade and problems for the elderly and infirm, but the experiment proved a complete success and the arrangement became permanent. However, it was 1982–3 before Market Place became completely traffic-free.

THE 1960s AND 1970s

Hall Street, 1965: right, part of the redevelopment area, and below, the same area after clearance. Some sort of redevelopment of this area had first been proposed in 1938. In October 1959 the town council approved a plan, and the first stage of work began in February 1962, with the levelling of Fisher Street car park. The redevelopment of Hall Street was phase two of the scheme, and began in March 1965. The council began compulsory purchase of over 6 acres of land in the Comprehensive Development Area in 1963. Objections were raised, but retailers were offered premises in the new developments, and manufacturers were offered alternative premises elsewhere. In justification of the scheme, the town clerk said 'Most of the centre of Dudley is of nineteenth-century development'. Many of the buildings in Hall Street were in poor

condition, and were not considered suitable, by the council, for modern shops. The aim of the redevelopment was very much in line with the current planning ideal of catering for traffic, deliveries, parked cars and pedestrians, but in separate places, allowing shoppers to walk around in freedom and relative safety.

Hawkesley Road, Russells Hall estate, 1966. Russells Hall housing estate was Dudley's largest postwar housing scheme. Building began in 1957 and half of the estate was completed by 1964. The first phase consisted of council housing, but two large plots were set aside for private development also. The houses were of varied design, intended to get away from the 'matchbox type dwellings' of other modern estates. The estate is built mainly on old pit land, and consequently all of the houses had to be built on reinforced concrete raft foundations to prevent movement.

Children playing outside Wychbury Court flats, 1967. Wychbury Court was the first high-rise block of flats to be completed in Dudley. Building began in 1963, after concrete had been injected into a coal seam under the site. The flats were officially opened on 24 November 1964, but the first tenants had moved in during the previous week. Council officials referred to the new blocks of eighty-six two-bedroomed flats as 'gifts from the gods'. In June 1965 this children's play area, with its model railway engine, was laid out, but by the end of the 1970s the council had decided that high-rise living was unsuitable for children, and families were no longer housed here.

Castle Street, Dudley, 1967. Castle Street was one of the borders of the Comprehensive Development Area, along with Fisher Street, Birmingham Street and part of Hall Street. Detailed plans for new shops to be built on the corner of Hall Street and Castle Street had been completed by the end of 1962, and demolition of the old shops began soon afterwards. The row on the right of this photograph was the result, with Cantor's furniture shop in the foreground, and Stanton's music shop at the other end. The street next to Cantor's is Hall Street, shortly before it was stopped up to make way for the pedestrianised Churchill Precinct.

Co-operative shop, High Street, 1969. This branch of the Co-op was celebrating its thirtieth anniversary in 1969, and to mark the occasion paid out triple dividends for three weeks. The building had been designed by Webb and Gray, Dudley architects, and was faced in very fashionable cream and blue tiles, made by the Stourbridge Glazed Brick Company. It had frontages on to High Street and Vicar Street, and a goods entrance in King Street. The store had departments selling almost everything except food, over four floors. It was opened on 16 December 1939 by Sir William Bradshaw JP, and closed in January 1983, following a merger between the Dudley and Birmingham Co-operative Societies.

Council houses in Green Park Road, 1969. These four houses, built in 1930, had just been drastically remodelled following flooding in July, at a cost of nearly £1,000 per house. The scheme was a pilot for the modernisation of a further 7,000 pre-war council houses. The Maintenance Section of the Housing Department had taken only six weeks to improve the kitchens, install an upstairs bathroom, retile the floors, completely rewire each house, insulate the roof spaces, provide extra lighting and power points, replace doors and window sills and redecorate. The finished houses were then opened to the public as 'show houses' to test their opinions. Regular transport was provided from Fisher Street bus station, and there was floodlighting for evening viewings.

Bainbridge Copnall and one of his six assistants working on the Churchill screen, 1967. The screen was the centrepiece of the Churchill Precinct and took two years to complete. It was 40 ft wide, consisted of seventeen glass panels, and weighed around 5 tons. The centre panel showed Winston Churchill in the ceremonial robes of a Knight of the Garter. Other panels showed scenes from the Second World War, the Houses of Parliament, Churchill's books and paintings, and some of his awards and honours. The base panels were of armour-plated glass, with the design built on top in pieces of, mainly Belgian, coloured glass. The screen was put in place in June 1968, 12 ft above the shopping mall.

Opening of the Churchill Precinct by Viscount Cobham, 8 September 1969. The precinct was built in two stages, forming phases two and three of the Hall Street/King Street redevelopment. Phase two, completed in August 1967, is the main thoroughfare of the precinct, which follows the line of the old Hall Street. This part was officially opened by the chairman of the General Purposes Committee of Dudley County Borough Council. The final phase extended the precinct towards King Street, and included Beattie's department store and the Churchill screen. The council was enormously proud of its new modern precinct, and the mayor, at the opening ceremony, said that 'This Churchill Precinct will never be outdated or obsolete'.

A meeting of Dudley Recorded Music Society, 18 March 1970. The first meeting of the society was held in March 1945 at the British Legion Club in Hall Street. The venue was moved to the upper gallery of the art gallery in St James's Road in 1949, and that is where this picture was taken. In 1969 the society could boast thirty-five members, each paying 15s a year, for forty-six meetings. At these meetings members would listen to records of various types of music; sometimes the programmes were presented by individual members themselves. The then secretary, Peter Hoggett, said: 'We cater for every taste, with the exception of pop.'

Volunteers on a 'Dudley Dig-In', October 1971. This event was organised by the Dudley Canal Trust and the Friends of the Black Country Museum, to clear the canal arm and basins leading off the Dudley Canal into the site of the Black Country Museum. A Leicestershire firm loaned a dredger free of charge, and this had already cleared the stretch of canal to a depth of 4 ft before the volunteers began to arrive on Saturday 1 October. The weekend was warm, and the organisers must have been pleased with the turn-out of over 200 volunteers on Saturday and over 250 on Sunday. They removed rubbish from the area, and generally worked on improving the site.

Birdcage Walk, 1972. The 'ultra-modern shopping precinct', as the *Dudley Herald* called it, was the first phase of the town centre redevelopment to be completed, and officially opened in April 1964. It took its name from the glass aviary situated at one end of it. This was kept stocked with parrots from Dudley Zoo from August 1964, when the first four macaws arrived, until November 1979, when the zoo's experts asked that they be rehoused. At the other end of the precinct, and just visible in this photograph, was a sculptured frieze by Bainbridge Copnall, representing local industry and education. Birdcage Walk could also boast a 240 ft long abstract mosaic, designed by Paul Rudall, Dudley Grammar School's art master.

Councillor Dr Katherine Rogers 'buying a brick' from Alison Bridgen for the Samaritans, Churchill Precinct, 22 January 1972. People were asked to contribute 10p towards building a centre for the charity, and the event raised £150. Kate Rogers, Dudley's first female mayor, was at this time serving her first term, of two, as mayor of Dudley. She was a councillor for Quarry Bank for thirty-four years in all, from 1952 to 1986, serving over the years with Staffordshire County Council, Brierley Hill Urban District Council, West Midlands County Council and Dudley County, later Metropolitan, Borough Council. She died in February 1989, aged eighty.

Bert Bissell, with one of the peace stones sent from Dudley to Hiroshima, Japan, 1972. Bert Bissell was a prominent local figure from the 1930s until his death, aged ninety-six, in November 1998. He established the Vicar Street Young Men's Bible Class, was Dudley's first probation officer, and campaigned for world peace. He was awarded the MBE in 1959, and the freedom of the boroughs of Dudley and Fort William. On VJ Day Bert Bissell and some of his Bible class began a peace cairn at the summit of Ben Nevis. Thereafter he made yearly peace pilgrimages up the mountain. This stone, made of Aberdeen granite, and a rock from Ben Nevis were installed in Hiroshima's Peace Park in May 1972.

A poster for Chipperfield's Circus, October 1972. This was the first circus to come to Dudley for eight years, and the zoo car park provided the venue for thirteen shows over the week of 23 to 28 October. A menagerie was also open daily. Chipperfield's was then the largest circus in Britain, and claimed more wild animals than all of the other circuses put together. Of the eighteen acts advertised seven involved performing animals, including Bengal tigers, lionesses, elephants and bears. The two-hour programme showcased the range of traditional circus acts. Ticket prices ranged from 25p to £1 for adults, half price for children.

Interior of Dudley Information Centre, Churchill Precinct, 1973. Part of Dudley Borough Council's library service, the centre was officially opened on 28 October 1972. It was established to answer a wide variety of questions from members of the public, provide information about activities and attractions in the area, and to sell tickets for local events. Most of the enquiries received in the 1970s related to council and government services, but the information centre also provided a tourist information service and was a local agent for the Heart of England Tourist Board. Miss Hilary Derricott, the first full-time information officer, is pictured at the desk.

A poster advertising the re-opening of Dudley canal tunnel, April 1973. The canal tunnel and Parkhead lock became the first stretch of officially abandoned inland waterway to be reintroduced to use, mainly thanks to the work of Dudley Canal Trust. Over a decade, bands of volunteers had gradually restored the canal until it was able to be reopened, under the codename TRAD (Tunnel Reopening at Dudley), by Sir Frank Price, chairman of the British Waterways Board, over the Easter weekend of 1973. The organisers had planned a ceremony based on original eighteenth- and nineteenth-century canal openings, and it was estimated that, despite the cold and wet weather, around ten thousand people and three hundred canal boats converged on the site.

Churchill Precinct, 1973, four years after its opening. The precinct had already run into problems – firstly with the floor, which was too slippery in wet weather; with vandalism, such as smashed windows; and a rooftop car park which was unpopular with the shop staff, who generally preferred to use the free car parks on King Street. In August 1970 a large piece of glass fell out of the Churchill screen, which was first covered and then removed for three years for repairs at a cost of £8,000. A glass roof was added to the precinct in 1993, after the council had sold the centre to LCP, as part of a £4 million refurbishment programme.

Dudley Tenants' Association join Dudley Trades Council's annual May Day march, 1973. Anyone who objected to the government's policies was invited to join the march through the town centre, and a rally at the Town Hall. Speakers included representatives of the Amalgamated Union of Engineering Workers and the Transport and General Workers Union and Dr Kate Rogers, who accused the government of broken promises on prices and taxes, called for nationalisation of land, more council houses and withdrawal from the Common Market. The Tenants' Association's involvement came about through their opposition to the Housing Finance Act, which meant increased rents for council housing. They even fielded candidates in the council elections in May 1973 on this issue.

The Queen and Prince Philip in Dudley, on 27 July 1977, as part of a whistle stop tour of the West Midlands, during Silver Jubilee year. Their day began in Wolverhampton, but they also visited Birmingham, Solihull, Coventry, Walsall and Sandwell. They were greeted in Dudley by cheering crowds, both on the streets and in Coronation Gardens, where the royal couple went on walkabout. They met several councillors and officials at the council house, and were given some pieces of crystal glass as a gift. They also viewed a collection of historic glass from Stourbridge and Brierley Hill – despite spending only twenty-seven minutes in Dudley in all!

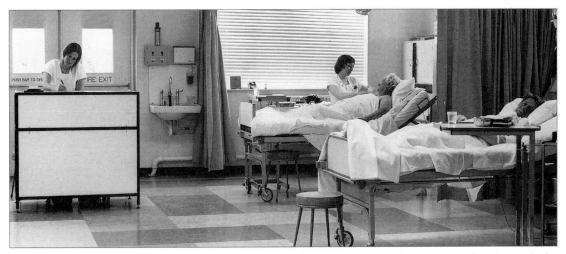

Burton Road Hospital, intensive therapy unit, c. 1977. This unit was opened in 1968, with only two beds. Within a year it had already made a name for itself by starting the heart of a Gornal man 195 times, and demand had become so great that a further extension, adding four more beds, was necessary. In June 1975 another extension, costing £17,000, was officially opened by Henry Marriott, a leading cardiologist from Atlanta, USA. The ITU had been doubled in size, to provide room for specialist equipment, two extra beds, a visitors' waiting room and a clinical room. It had already cost £40,000 and most of that had come from charitable contributions, including Dudley Mayor's Fund.

CMT Industrial Supplies Ltd, 1977. This company was established early in the 1970s as a distributor of asbestos, rubber and plastics for industry. It later diversified into protective clothing, structural materials, industrial fastenings and conveyor belts. The company's centre of operations at this time was on Halesowen Road, Netherton. This photograph is of the interior of the engineering insulation division, where asbestos was machined and treated, which was on the Corngreaves Industrial Estate in Cradley Heath. It was, however, included in the 1977 Dudley borough guide. All divisions of the group relocated to Cradley Heath in the mid-1980s.

A procession to mark the official legalisation of the group ministry of Dudley's seven Anglican churches, 1979. The parade, led by cross bearers and banners representing all of the central group churches, marched from St Edmund's to St Thomas's ('Top') church. Also taking part in the parade was the mayor, Councillor Mrs Gwen Homer, and her consort, the bishops of Dudley and Worcester, Anglican clergy and congregations, ministers of other denominations, and the Salvation Army band, which played hymns that the procession sang. Around five hundred people were in church for the service of commissioning, which was taken jointly by the Rt Rev. Robin Woods, Bishop of Worcester and the Rt Rev. Anthony Dumper, Bishop of Dudley.

7. Into the New Millennium: the 1980s and 1990s

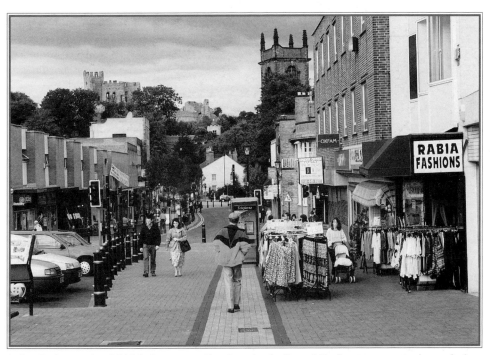

Rabia Fashions, April 1998. Some consider that the decline of Dudley town centre began before the opening of the final phase of the Merry Hill shopping centre in 1989, but this undoubtedly accelerated it, as High Street names, especially the multiple stores, deserted the town centre. Many properties fell vacant and the discount stores moved in. Refurbishment schemes were introduced to try and halt the decline. The market does, however, remain popular and the town centre is usually very busy. There seemed to have been surprisingly little change over the previous few years on the section of Castle Street seen here, Rabia Fashions, Oxfam and Braggs Baker having been there since about 1994. Plans dated 1993 show Etams, Hudsons and Rumbelows along this section.

Introduction

In the 1980s Dudley seemed to be a town in terminal decline. The economic problems suffered by the nation were particularly acute here. Unemployment hit new postwar highs, and many established town centre stores disappeared. By the end of the decade, though, there was some cause for optimism, and now, at the end of the 1990s, the town seems to be enjoying better fortunes once again.

The decline in heavy industry, which had begun in the 1970s, accelerated in the early 1980s. Dudley had traditionally relied heavily on manufacturing industries and was hit particularly hard. In 1978 nearly 50 per cent of jobs in the borough were in these industries, while nationally the figure was less than a third. At its height, unemployment in the borough as a whole was at 18 per cent, above the national and regional average, and many old-established firms closed down or relocated during this period. The situation was made considerably worse when Round Oak Steel Works at Brierley Hill closed in 1982. Despite this, Dudley failed to obtain full steel closure status, and therefore was not eligible for assistance under the European Regional Development Fund or Assisted Area status.

In 1981 the number of people unemployed in Britain rose to 2½ million for the first time since the 1930s. This represented 10.4 per cent of the working population. In Dudley the total was nearly 13 per cent, and rising. In July 1981 the government announced the establishment of the first Enterprise Zones, which were intended to breathe new life into ailing areas. Dudley Enterprise Zone was amongst them, and covered 300 acres in Netherton and Brierley Hill. A second Dudley (Round Oak) Enterprise Zone was designated in October 1984. Businesses were given incentives to move into the zones, such as exemption from rates and taxes and greater planning freedom, which were to last for ten years. In Dudley's case the land was entirely privately owned, and owners were required to sign an agreement to develop, or face the threat of a compulsory purchase order. There was much optimism about this new scheme, but in fact it had very little impact initially. In the first year twenty-six firms were established in the Enterprise Zone, but only nine were completely new, and nine established firms within the zone either closed or left the area. In total, after the first year, there was a net increase of only four jobs.

The Merry Hill Centre in Brierley Hill was developed in five phases between 1986 and 1989, and has had a significant impact on Dudley town centre. Several of the larger High Street shops closed their Dudley outlets, and relocated at Merry Hill, and discount stores began to take over. In many cases premises remained empty, and the number of retail outlets in the town centre declined considerably between 1987 and 1993. Traffic and parking problems also played a part in this decline. Some stores, such as Beattie's, however, have remained, as has the market, and attempts to improve the centre and attract shoppers back have met with some success in recent years.

Dudley's appearance has continued to change in other ways as well. The market was given a facelift in the early 1980s, when the stalls were replaced and the cobbles removed. The Churchill Precinct, built by the council in the 1960s, was sold in 1991 to London and Cambridge Properties, on condition that they carry out refurbishment work on the somewhat outdated centre. This was done in 1993, at a cost of £4 million. A glass roof and automatic doors at the entrances were added, as well as new decor. Some of Dudley's historic buildings have been lost in recent years, such as Dudley Girls' High School which had occupied its position in Priory Road since 1910 and was demolished in 1996, and Burton Road Hospital, formerly Dudley Union workhouse, which was knocked down in 1994. The site of the school is currently being used as a car park, while that of the hospital has been redeveloped for housing. In July 1999 some much more modern landmarks also disappeared – two of the blocks of multi-storey flats at Eve Hill.

The Dudley Southern Bypass, first put forward in the 1980s, opened in October 1999, five months ahead of schedule. This should solve some of the traffic problems which Dudley has long experienced. As part of this project, an area on Birmingham Road is being developed as an entertainment complex, to be known as Castle Gate. It will contain the first new cinema built in Dudley since the 1930s, as well as a health club, hotel, pub and restaurant.

So Dudley enters the next century with more change to look forward to – Dudley Southern Bypass, Castle Gate and new housing at Eve Hill, to name just a few of the current projects. In the midst of it all, though, the castle and Market Place remain, central to the town still, as they were at the turn of the last century.

Inside a Sikh temple, Dudley, *c.* 1980, from a series of photographs entitled 'Impressions of a Black Country Community'. The first Sikh temple in Dudley was opened in Wellington Road in 1970. It was housed in a former Methodist church, which had been acquired and furnished at a cost of about £9,000. At this time it was one of only about sixty such temples in the country. The opening ceremony was attended by the mayor and the assistant high commissioner for India, along with about three hundred people. In 1970 it was estimated that around two hundred and fifty Sikh families lived in Dudley, many of whom came from the Punjab and spoke Punjabi. By 1982 around 4½ per cent of the population of the borough belonged to ethnic minority communities.

Millard's Brewery (Gipsies Tent public house), with Hanson's Brewery chimney behind, 1981. The Little Model Brewery at the rear of the Gipsies Tent was built in about 1886 when Millard needed to expand the existing brewery, because of increased demand for his home brew. The new building consisted of a four-storey tower with a block on each side. Although brewing ceased in 1961, the derelict remains of the brewery can still be seen today. Hansons Brewery, which was behind the Model Brewery and whose chimney can be seen here, was closed by Wolverhampton & Dudley Breweries in 1993, and the building demolished in 1994. Hansons beer is now brewed in Wolverhampton, and a Netto supermarket stands on that site.

Impressions of Dudley, a Black Country community, c. 1980, showing a traditional pub card game. Public houses have been a focal point in their local communities since the nineteenth century, providing a meeting place for social gatherings, organising and developing recreational activities as well as providing a convivial place where working men especially could relax. Social and economic change during this century has altered the concept of the pub: in the early part of the century many were of the 'spit and sawdust' type, but by the 1980s women were to be found in the lounge bars. Many small breweries have been taken over by regional ones, although a few independent breweries have survived, providing 'real ale' for aficionados.

A group of Blue Coat Secondary School pupils, 1981. This picture was used in the school's 1981–2 prospectus to illustrate the wide range of extra-curricular activities available. As well as the computer club, students could join clubs for photography, electronics, chess, pottery, woodwork and metal work, various sports, and the Adventure Club, which encouraged participation in the Duke of Edinburgh Awards scheme. Blue Coat had offered computer studies at O-level/CSE since the mid-1970s, and in 1981 an introduction to computers was taught to twelve to fourteen year olds as well. The school closed in 1989 and became part of Castle High School.

Dudley's mayor, Councillor David Ranceford-Hadley, and deputy mayor Councillor David Caunt, trying out new technology at an exhibition of commodities purchased by the council, 1982. David Ranceford-Hadley was elected mayor in May 1982, having served as a local councillor for Stourbridge and Pedmore since 1969 and deputy mayor in 1981–2. Dudley Council had purchased its first computer, a forty column installation from International Computers and Tabulators Ltd, in 1961, after a report had demonstrated the need to mechanise the accounting process. A new computer was needed to tackle the workload after the borough's 1966 expansion. This was purchased in 1970 and housed above the fire station in Tower Street, in a room of 4,500 square feet!

WYKO Ltd, engineering shop, 1982. WYKO was established in 1962, by Philip White, to make and distribute engineering spares and consumables. From this base, the company became involved in producing and distributing tyre building equipment, gears and gearboxes, hydraulic presses, specialised bearings, and power transmission components. During the 1970s and '80s the Dudley-based company also established itself in West Germany, South Africa and the USA. The company still has works in Dudley and Halesowen, and 106 British industrial distribution branches in total. It employs 2,300 staff, mainly in the UK. Currently a management buy-out is under discussion, valuing the company at £92.2 million.

Market Place, shortly after the completion of refurbishment work, 1983. During the previous year the drainage and sewerage systems were improved, and pedestrianisation introduced between New Street and Stone Street. At the same time benches were provided in Market Place, as well as permanent flower displays, litter bins and ornamental cast-iron bollards to block off the road. The total cost was around £90,000. The market itself also received a facelift. The original cobbles were replaced with flat concrete paving stones, and the wooden framed stalls removed to the Black Country Museum. While the work was carried out, the market was temporarily relocated in Stone Street.

View from the top of Dudley Castle to Castle Hill, February 1998. The zoo entrance, with its waved roof, can be seen on the right, and to the left of it, one of the castle's gatehouses. In the foreground is the chair lift. This was opened on 11 May 1957, the 21st anniversary of the Dudley Zoological Society, and was the first of its kind in the country. It originally had 50 seats, and could carry up to 650 people per hour up the 200 ft slope from the entrance to the elephant house – a walk of around ¼ mile. On the other side of the road is the former Odeon cinema and on the left of this photograph, the Station hotel.

A concert by Dudley Schools Orchestra in the town hall, *c.* 1984. This orchestra was formed in 1968 by Mr D.I. Lewis, Dudley's music adviser. All schoolchildren in the county borough were eligible for membership, on a voluntary basis, and there were no auditions. Mr Lewis ran the orchestra jointly with Mr K. Farmer, head of peripatetic instrumental teachers, for many years. When Dudley Borough was enlarged into its present metropolitan district, the format of the orchestra changed. Three orchestras ran in parallel, one in Dudley, one in Halesowen and a third in Stourbridge, which each met weekly. From these groups a senior borough orchestra was formed after selection by audition.

The City of Birmingham Symphony Orchestra, performing at Dudley Town Hall, *c.* 1985. Dudley Town Hall is the largest of the borough's five civic halls, seating 1,060 for concerts. Its acoustics are said to be excellent, and Lord Menuhin described it as 'one of the finest halls in the country'. The CBSO are regular visitors, and have used it to make many of their recordings.

A computer controlled autoclave in operation at Herman Smith Hitco's plant, 1983. This company had only been open for a short time when it invested more than £100,000 in this machine. It was believed to be one of the first micro-computer controlled autoclaves, and one of the most advanced in the world. It was essentially a large pressurised oven, used for curing resins. The company later became F.R. Hitco, and built a new factory and office complex in the Dudley Enterprise Zone. It specialised in advanced composite structures for aerospace, commercial and industrial applications, and was recognised by the Ministry of Defence in 1983.

A locomotive arriving at Dudley to collect the last freightliner train, 26 September 1986. Dudley's Freightliner Terminal was opened to traffic on 6 November 1967. It cost around £250,000 to build and could deal with up to twelve trains per day. The new depot proved so successful that a second one was opened in Birmingham in 1970 to take some of the workload. In July 1981 closure proposals were first announced by Freightliner Ltd, who wanted to transfer Dudley's traffic to Birmingham, despite the fact that Dudley was the fourth most profitable terminal in the country, while Birmingham made the third biggest loss. The Dudley depot managed to survive until September 1986, when it was finally closed and its remaining staff transferred to Birmingham.

Mobile library, *c.* 1986. Until 1966 Dudley library service consisted of a central library and service points at Netherton, Woodside, Dudley Wood and Lodge Farm, but it had no mobile library. Following the boundary changes in 1966 under which Coseley and Brierley Hill were incorporated into the borough, the library service purchased a secondhand vehicle from Herefordshire which went into service in May 1966. A replacement vehicle was purchased the following year and by 1975 there were three mobiles. The mobile library served the borough's outlying areas and also its schools, and soon replaced the dilapidated Lodge Farm Library. Reduced to one van by 1986, and in light of falling issues and financial cutbacks, the mobile library service was axed in May 1991.

A flyer for the first National Cycle Festival, 1987. This event, organised by Dudley council and several major cycling associations, was held at Himley Hall on 27 and 28 June, and attracted around 12,000 visitors. Amateur and professional cyclists from across the country competed in various races, including cycle speedway, cyclocross, a 140 mile road race over the two days, and a 400 metre sprint for penny farthings. There was controversy when the BMX champion of champions course was deemed to be too dangerous. Several of the 900 competitors fell at one of the sharpest bends, and two ended up in hospital with broken bones. The race had to be delayed for several hours while the course was rebuilt.

SEE YOU AT THE

NATIONAL CYCLE FESTIVAL
DUDLEY 1987

Himley Hall Park, nr. Dudley, West Midlands
Saturday 27th & Sunday 28th June

Bringing you Cycling for All

National Cycle Festival, 1988. The second event was again based at Himley Hall park and took place over the weekend of 2 and 3 July. The festival included a charity cyclathon, cycle speedway, a cavalcade of cycle history, and indoor races, as well as the two day, 185-mile road race, the Dudley section of which is shown here. This part of the circuit took in Market Place, Wolverhampton Street, Priory Street and New Street in Dudley town centre. The race was judged an overwhelming success and culminated in an exciting finish, with the winner being decided in the last half mile. He was John Rimmer of Zenith Cycle Club, and he beat Darren Worsdale of West Midlands Centre of Excellence by just two seconds. The organisers declared the second National Cycle Festival a success, despite a much lower than expected turnout and the cancellation of two races. The visitor figures for 1988 were only around four thousand, a third of the previous year's total. This was largely blamed on the absence of the national BMX race from that year's programme. The cyclocross and grass track events had to be cancelled because of a lack of entrants.

Above: The offices of ACT, computer software
company, *c.* 1987. This firm was originally based
in Halesowen, but moved to Netherton in about
1986. In the mid-1980s they were the largest
micro-computer software company in Britain, and
had developed both the Apricot and Sirius I
machines in the borough. The decline in
manufacturing industry in the 1980s hit Dudley
very hard. At its height, unemployment in the
borough was running at 18 per cent. This has
now greatly improved, and the industrial and
commercial base of the borough has diversified to
include more jobs in new, high-tech. industries,
such as this one, and the service sector.

Right: A poster for an Asian Fashion Show,
13 March 1990. This event was organised by
Dudley One World and Dudley Leisure Services,
in association with Zara Fashion Modes, one of
Britain's top Asian fashion houses. At this event
they were able to show their latest styles, with
more than seventy outfits on display, modelled by
Dudley girls of various ethnic backgrounds. The
second half of the show included a display of
Bhangra dancing and live music, featuring
Gucharon Mal, and his Nachdar Sansaar
Dancers. Dudley One World aims to promote
greater multicultural understanding and
appreciation through events such as this.

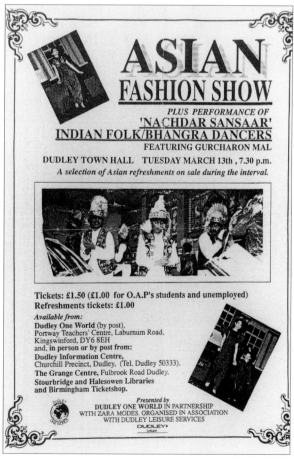

Thomas Jones's Fun Fair, Stone Street, 19 December 1990. This week-long fair was organised by the council's town centre development sub-committee in a bid to attract customers to the town centre in the run up to Christmas. It was opened by the mayor and mayoress at 12 noon on Monday 19 December, and rides were free for the first hour. The fair was set up in Stone Street car park, Stone Street itself and Market Place, and coincided with late night shopping, which included the market stalls. It was not a success. Traders reported a 25 per cent fall in takings in comparison with the same week in the preceding year, and customers complained about the noise and lack of parking.

VJ Day anniversary celebrations, August 1995. A parade and open air service in Coronation Gardens, took place on 20 August in a civic tribute to commemorate the fiftieth anniversary of VJ Day, the end of the war in Japan. Over 1,000 people attended the service which started at 3 p.m., and addresses were made by peace campaigner Bert Bissell and the mayor's chaplain. More than 200 war veterans proudly wore their uniforms and medals and braved the heat to take part in the parade, which started in the Market Place and culminated at Coronation Gardens via Stone Street, Priory Street, Priory Road and Ednam Road. They were led by 77-year-old Arthur Grove who carried the Burma Star Association standard.

The demolition of Dudley Girls' High School, Priory Road, February 1996. Its demise came about following the amalgamation of the Girls' High School with the Grammar School in St James's Road to form the Dudley School, becoming Castle High later. When a new £4 million extension was opened in St James's Road and the pupils transferred, the bulk of the Priory Road site was no longer used; only the adjacent sports hall was still needed until a new one could be built. Vandalism was rampant and it was costing money for maintenance and security, so the school decided to make a separate access for the sports hall and demolish the bulk of the buildings. The site was cleared and the area is now, temporarily, a long-stay car park.

Priory Road from the Civic Gardens, Ednam Road, 1996, showing Dudley Girls' High School and Eve Hill flats left of centre, now demolished. The Civic Gardens were laid out by Dudley Council between 1935 and 1939 as a public amenity. A statue of Apollo, reputed to be the guardian of civic enterprise, was donated by E.J. Thompson, and erected there in 1939. In 1980 some councillors expressed concern that this residential area of large houses was changing to commercial use and eroding its character. No. 10 Ednam Road, a four-bedroom detached house with swimming pool, was being sold and approval was being sought to turn it into a surgery.

The housing development on the former Burton Road hospital site, April 1997. The photograph above is of Ashdale Park, Dibdale Road; the one below shows Bishops Lodge. The demolition of Burton Road Hospital in 1994 created a potential site for redevelopment covering 13 acres. It was offered for sale in September 1995, and listed as suitable for residential development. Dudley Council approved plans for the building of 253 three- and four-bedroom houses, together with any associated roads and sewers, on land off Dibdale Road and Deepdale Lane on 16 November 1995. The subsequent massive housing estate has been developed by a number of companies; Allen Homes were advertising houses for sale in Ashdale Park from May 1996. Prices ranged from £49,000 for a two-bedroom semi-detached house to £89,000 for a four-bedroom detached house.

Dudley College of Technology, Mons Hill Annexe, October 1997. Formerly the Wrens Nest Secondary School, it opened in 1965 and was renamed Mons Hill School following the introduction of comprehensive education in the borough in September 1975. In this same year a full-time community tutor had been appointed to develop youth, community and adult education services in the area. The school was closed in July 1990 when falling numbers on the school roll made it no longer viable and most pupils and staff were transferred to the nearby Coseley School. The school roll showed that 3,518 pupils had been through the doors. The building was later taken over by Dudley College, who in 1993 opened a £2.3 million extension here.

Scots Green junction with Stourbridge Road, as work gets underway on the Dudley Southern Bypass, 1998. Work was started in March 1998 and was completed in October 1999, at an estimated cost of £55 million. The bypass was first proposed in 1987 in order to improve access and increase the capacity for heavy traffic to the Enterprise Zone and Pensnett Trading Estate, to improve traffic safety in Dudley town centre and to link the proposed new developments at Castle Hill with the Merry Hill Centre. This 2-mile dual carriageway now runs from Holly Hall to the junction of the A461 with Tipton Road. The route was planned carefully so that there would be minimal effect on the environment.

Burton Road fire station, April 1999. Proposals for a new state of the art fire station to replace the Tower Street station were unveiled on 23 October 1996. The old fire station was in need of a £500,000 refurbishment, and for a number of years the congested roads in the town centre had caused problems for emergency vehicles. An out-of-town site at the junction of The Broadway and Burton Road had been found, next to the ambulance station, and Dudley Council gave approval in December for the 1¾-acre site, provided the West Midlands Fire Authority paid for road improvements, traffic lights and new signs along Burton Road. The first sod was cut by the mayor, Councillor Mary Hill, on 28 July 1997, and after considerable stabilisation work because of mine workings the £2.2 million station, built by Try Construction of Birmingham, was opened in April 1999 by the chairman of the West Midlands Fire and Defence Authority, Councillor Peter Bilson.

Eve Hill Flats, April 1999. At noon on 18 July 1999 two of these twenty-storey blocks of flats, Prince of Wales Court and Millfield Court, were demolished in front of huge crowds. The flats had fallen into disrepair, and after consultations with residents it was decided to demolish two blocks but to renovate the third, Butterfield Court. Tenants had likened conditions to The Bronx, and 166 out of 170 residents in the blocks voted for demolition. There were 118 flats in each block and the residents were given compensation and also given priority for rehousing on other council estates.

Demolition of Eve Hill Flats. The honour of signalling the demolition went to businessman Mike Charteris, who won the raffle organised by the Rotary Club to raise money for Russells Hall Hospital's cardiac unit. On the day of the demolition 400 nearby residents were evacuated as a safety precaution, but the only casualty reported was of a fledgling dove falling out of a tree in St James's church graveyard. Over 8,000 tons of rubble were created, as the buildings collapsed like a pack of cards in about three seconds. This is to be recycled and used as hard-core for new housing. Between 90 and 115 homes will be built on the site, in a mix of private and rented accommodation, and the nearby open land is to be renovated once the rubble has been removed. At noon a klaxon sounded to warn of the impending event: with one minute to go a flare was let off as first the Prince of Wales Court and then Millfield Court collapsed as the Controlled Demolition Group set off 50 kg of explosives using 1,000 detonators. There were reported to have been over 2,000 people watching the spectacle, in a carnival atmosphere, and as the second building crumbled the cheers rang out.

Acknowledgements

Aerofilms, Allen & Bott, Mr B. Bawden, Cheltenham, Beddard, *Birmingham Post & Mail*, Mr T.E. Bredee, Mr J. Brough, Mr A.J. Bytheway, Executors of Mr W. Camm, The headteacher, Castle High School, Dudley (for photographs of Dudley Grammar School, Girls' High School and Blue Coat School), Central Press, CMT Industrial Supplies Ltd, County Express, Mrs. Davies, Dudley Area Health Authority, Dudley Camera Club (formerly Dudley Photographic Society), Dudley Conservative Club, Dudley MBC, DuPont Group (for Revo Electric Co.), *Express & Star*, C. Fenton, Mr. Fereday, Graphic Photo Union, Mrs J. Holl, Imperial War Museum, Mr S. Jeavons, Mr C. Lavender, C.N.F. Lewis, Mr H. Madelin, Mary Stevens Hospice, Stourbridge (for use of Dr Kate Rogers's photographs), Mr W.H. Massey, Midland United Newspapers Ltd, Mr M. Pearson, Mr A. Perry, Mr F. Power, Minister and trustees of Providence Methodist Chapel, Darby End, Mr D.F. Radmore, Mr Richards, Mr R. Round, St John Ambulance Brigade (Dudley branch), St Thomas's with St Luke's Parochial Church Council, Miss Simpson, Mr Spettigue, Miss J. Taylor, Taylor's Press Services, Toc H, Netherton (men's branch), Topical Press Agency, Mr H. Vanes, Miss Wade, Mr S. White, Ned Williams, Mr T. Woolams.

The authors would like to thank especially: all other members of Dudley Archives and Local History Service staff for their support, and Mr Frank Power, photographer.

Bibliography

Serials

Blocksidge's *Dudley Almanacks*
Dudley Herald
Kelly's Directories of Worcestershire
St John's church, Kates Hill, parish magazines
The Blackcountryman
Black Country Bugle
The Dudleian, school magazine of Dudley Grammar School
The Cornflower, school magazine of Dudley Girls' High School
The Sentinel, unofficial chronicle of Dudley's ARP, January 1940
Local History newscuttings volumes
Leisure and Recreation newsuttings books
Dudley News
Dudley and Black Country Life
Dudley Chronicle

Printed

Chronicle of the Twentieth Century, ed. Derrik Mercer, 1988
Sutton, Richard, *Motor Mania: Stories from a Motoring Century*, 1996
Burgess-Wise, David, *Automobile Archaeology*, 1981
Miller's *Collectors' Cars Price Guide*, 1995–96
Williams, Ned, *The Co-op in Birmingham and the Black Country*, 1993
Richards, John, *The Pubs and Breweries of the Old Dudley Borough*, 1989
Souvenir of Dudley Pageant, 1908, reprinted from Herald Series
Dudley County Borough, *Programme and Souvenir of the Opening of the New Central Library*, 1909
Dudley CB, later MBC official guides
Official programme of the visit of HRH the Prince of Wales to Dudley, 1923
Chignell, W.R., *History of Worcestershire County Cricket Club, 1844–1950*, ?1950
Tipton C.B. Official Guide, 1956
Dudley Girls' High School prospectus, *c.* 1928
Souvenir brochure, Scrim Manufacturing Co. Ltd.
The Great War: A Black Country Perspective, Dudley MBC Planning and Leisure Dept. 1996
Market Sale: Souvenir Programme, Dudley and District Prisoners of War Fund, 1918
Hodgson, Godfrey, *People's Century*, 1995
Tames, Richard, *1900–1919: Picture History of the 20th century*
Tames, Richard, *Picture History of The 20th Century: The 1920s*, 1991
Freeman, Charles, *Portrait of a Decade: The 1930s*, 1990
Bowles, D., *Official guide and map to the Dudley Zoo*, 1949
Concentrated Conservatism; election leaflet, 1949
County Express, *Silver Jubilee 1952–1977; a County Express souvenir*, 1977
Douglas, Alton, et al, *The Black Country at war*, 1984
Fyson, Nance Lui, *Growing up in the post-war forties*, 1985
Fyson, Nance Lui, *Portrait of a decade*, 1985
Guttery, D.R., *The Queens Own Worcestershire Hussars, 1922–1956*, 1958
Hobley, L. F., *Since 1945*, 1977
Mackenzie, S.P., *The Home Guard*, 1995
Parsons, Harold, *Murder and mystery in the Black Country*, 1989
A short history of the units administered by the Staffordshire Territorial & Auxiliary Forces Association, 1950
Staffordshire County Council, *Staffordshire county civil defence; official handbook*, 1943